Saints CHRONICLES

Collection 3

SOPHIA INSTITUTE PRESS
Manchester, NH

SOPHIA
INSTITUTE PRESS

Text and Images Copyright © 2018 Sophia Institute

Printed in the United States of America.

Sophia Institute Press®
Box 5284, Manchester, NH 03108
1-800-888-9344

www.SophiaInstitute.com

Sophia Institute Press® is a registered trademark of Sophia Institute.

No part of this book may be reproduced, stored in a retrieval system, or transmitted in any form, or by any means, electronic, mechanical, photocopying, or otherwise, without the prior written permission of the publisher, except by a reviewer, who may quote brief passages in a review.

Names, persons, places, and incidents featured in this publication are based on historical fact but have been subject to author and artist discretion for dramatic purposes. All text, except when specifically cited, has been written by the author, not to be mistaken for actual historical documentation.

The Saints Chronicles Collection 1, ISBN: 9781622826742
The Saints Chronicles Collection 2, ISBN: 9781622826766
The Saints Chronicles Collection 3, ISBN: 9781622826797
The Saints Chronicles Collection 4, ISBN: 9781622826803

Library of Congress Cataloging-in-Publication Data

Title: The saints chronicles. Collection 1. Saint Patrick, Saint Jerome Emiliani, Saint Elizabeth Ann Seton, Saint Henry Morse, Saint Joan of Arc.
Description: Manchester, NH : Sophia Institute Press, [2018]
Identifiers: LCCN 2018038952 | ISBN 9781622826742 (pbk. : alk. paper)
Subjects: LCSH: Christian saints–Biography–Comic books, strips, etc. | Christian martyrs–Biography–Comic books, strips, etc. | Catholics–Biography–Comic books, strips, etc. | Patrick, Saint, 373?-463? –Comic books, strips, etc. | Jerome Emiliani, Saint, 1486-1537 –Comic books, strips, etc. | Seton, Elizabeth Ann, Saint, 1774-1821 –Comic books, strips, etc. | Morse, Henry, Saint, 1595-1645 –Comic books, strips, etc. | Joan, of Arc, Saint, 1412-1431 –Comic books, strips, etc. | Graphic novels.
Classification: LCC BX4655.3 .S255 2018 | DDC 282.092/2 [B] –dc23
LC record available at https://lccn.loc.gov/2018038952

THE Saints CHRONICLES
Collection 3

Saint Antony of Padua...................... 2
Saint Ava..24
Saint Samson....................................46
Saint Bernadette..............................68
Saint Charles Lwanga......................90

What do you think God's will is for your life?

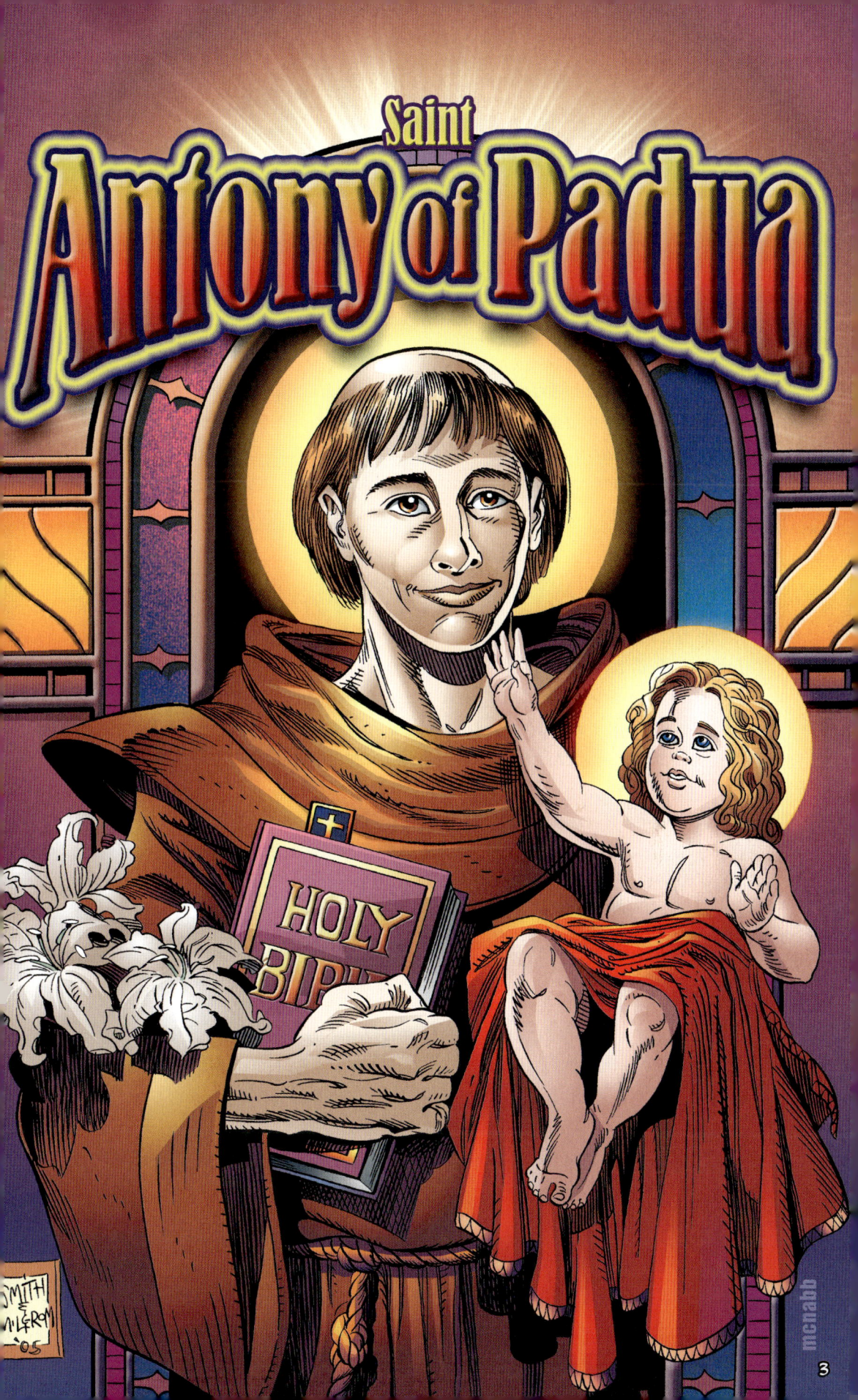

Antony of Padua

Antony of Padua, beloved saint of the Catholic church, was a man dedicated to his faith and to the practice of the Franciscan ministry throughout Europe during the thirteenth century. St. Antony was a devout member of the Franciscan Order who was revered for his immense knowledge of the Bible, his ability to preach, and his passion for reaching lost and lonely souls.

St. Antony was baptized with the name Ferdinand. Young Ferdinand was a typical religious man living in Spain; he joined a monastery and devoted his life to education. Ferdinand's life took an exciting and unexpected turn at age twenty-five when he received the call to become a martyr. He changed his name to Antony in 1221 in order to mark his entrance into the Order of the Friars Minor.

Although he lived during the time of St. Francis and was known in the Franciscan order for his many gifts, St. Antony never spoke with St. Francis of Assisi. However, the two shared many similar characteristics. Each was a man of God who chose to live in poverty, felt compassion for the friendless, and spread God's message to thousands of people.

St. Antony was canonized within a year of his death by Pope Gregory IX. In 1946, Pope Pius XII declared him a Doctor of the Church.

~

{Producer} Daniel Burton ~ {Editorial} Kimberly Black
{Story} Jen Murvin Edwards ~ {Pencils} Tod Smith
{Inks} Al Milgrom ~ {Colors} Mark McNabb
{Letters | Design} Jeff Dawidowski

The next evening...

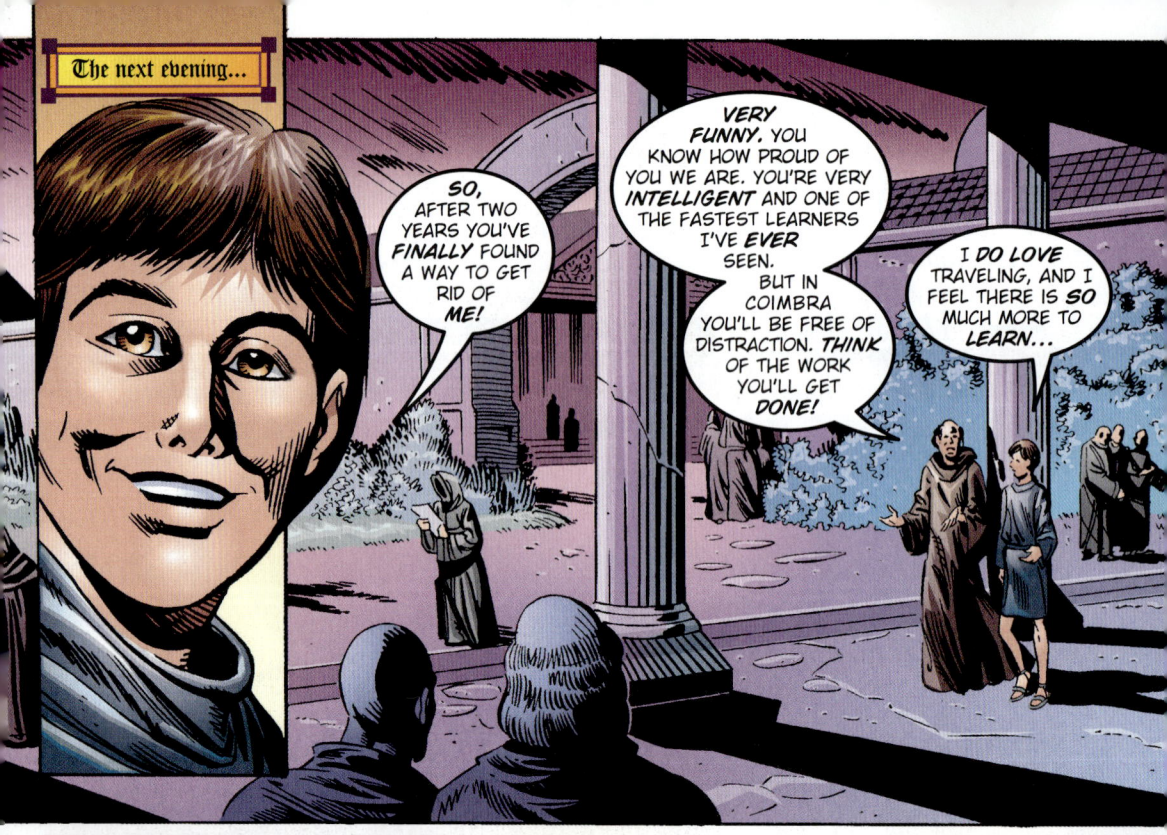

SO, AFTER TWO YEARS YOU'VE FINALLY FOUND A WAY TO GET RID OF ME!

VERY FUNNY. YOU KNOW HOW PROUD OF YOU WE ARE. YOU'RE VERY INTELLIGENT AND ONE OF THE FASTEST LEARNERS I'VE EVER SEEN. BUT IN COIMBRA YOU'LL BE FREE OF DISTRACTION. THINK OF THE WORK YOU'LL GET DONE!

I DO LOVE TRAVELING, AND I FEEL THERE IS SO MUCH MORE TO LEARN...

I KNOW YOU ARE YOUNG, BUT I HAVE FAITH THAT THERE IS A LIFE OF GREAT WORKS AHEAD OF YOU.

IF YOU GO TO COIMBRA, YOU WILL NEED TO BE FOCUSED IN YOUR STUDIES AND LEARN AS MUCH AS YOU POSSIBLY CAN.

USE YOUR GIFTS, FERDINAND. GOD HAS BLESSED YOU GREATLY, AND HE WILL USE YOU IF YOU LET HIM.

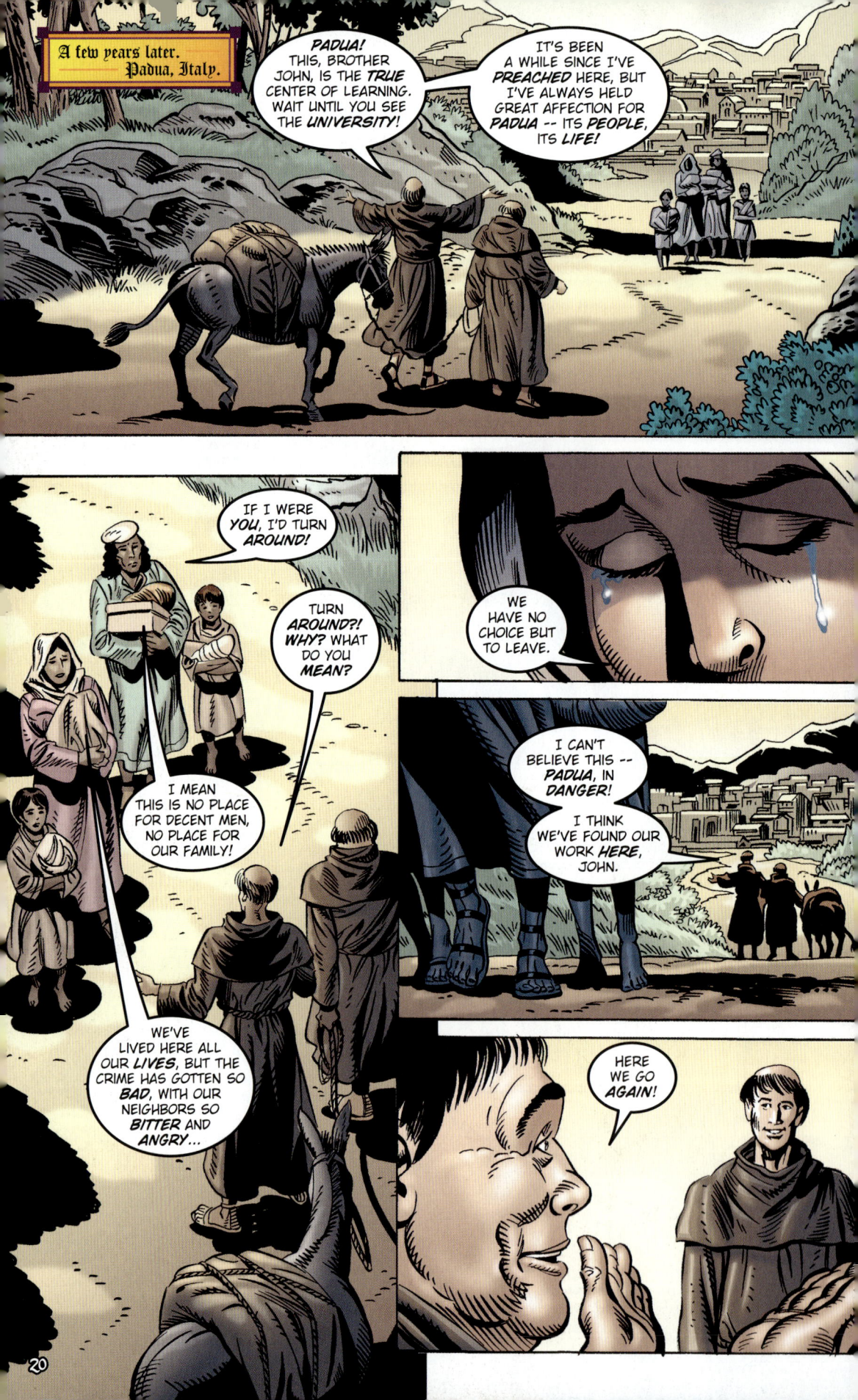

A Saint's Journey

1195. St. Antony is born and baptized with the name Fernando Martins de Bulhões (Ferdinand, in English). His early education is from the clergy of the cathedral in Lisbon, Portugal.

1210. St Antony joins regular canons of St. Augustine near Lisbon.

1212. He transfers to the priory at Coimbra, which is the capital of Portugal at the time.

1220. Don Pedro arrives with relics of the Franciscans who suffered martyrdom.

1222. St. Antony delivers his awe-inspiring address at Forli in the Minorite convent.

1226. His final home is Padua where he sees much fruit from his labors. He is greatly loved, and his sermons are listened to by enormous congregations.

June 13, 1231. The young Paduan, St. Antony, receives the last rites and passes to his eternal reward. St. Antony is canonized within a year of his death by Pope Gregory IX.

1946. Pope Pius XII declares him a Doctor of the Church.

Lisbon, Portugal, the year 1212. Canons of St. Augustine.

Eight years later. Priory of Coimbra.

San Paolo, Italy. Small community of the Friars Minor.

A few years later. Padua, Italy.

When did you know something was true, even though you couldn't see it at the time?

Saint AVA

The life of **St. Ava** is one of mystery and shrouded in **legend**.

Verified facts are few. **Here** is what we **know** for sure:

She was a member of the **Frankish Royal Family** and related to **King Pepin** of Belgium.

Born **blind**, she was later **believed** to have been miraculously **cured** through the efforts of **St. Rainfredis**.

She entered a **convent** at Dinart, Hainault, became a **Benedictine Nun**, and was elected as **abbess**.

Her feast day is **April 29th**.

This is **her story**.

PRODUCER:
DANIEL BURTON

EDITORIAL:
KIMBERLY BLACK

STORY:
TERRY COLLINS

ART:
SERGIO CARIELLO &
CLAUDE ST. AUBIN

COLORS:
CRAIG SCHUTT &
JEREMY MOHLER

LETTERS / DESIGNS:
KEITH BAHRENBURG

"BLESSED ARE THOSE WHO DO NOT SEE...

YET BELIEVE."
-- JOHN 20:29

GOOD DAY TO YOU, CHILD.

AND TO YOU AS WELL.

MAY I JOIN YOU?

OF COURSE.

THANK YOU.

I WAS TOLD I MIGHT FIND YOU IN THE GARDEN.

I LIKE IT OUT HERE.

REALLY? AND WHY IS THAT?

"ONE DAY, AS JESUS WENT ALONG A PATH, HE SAW A **MAN BLIND** FROM **BIRTH**. STOPPING TO OFFER ASSISTANCE, ONE OF THE **DISCIPLES** SPOKE."

Rabbi, who **sinned**, this man or his parents, that he was **born blind?**

Neither this man nor his parents **sinned**. He was born blind so that **God's works** might be revealed in **him**.

We must do the **works** of **Him who sent Me** while it is day.

Night is coming, when **no one** can **work**.

"I am the man ... I am he."

"How then were your eyes opened?"

"Yes! How?"

"The man they call **Jesus**. He made **mud** and put it on my eyes. He **told** me to go to Siloam and **wash**."

"**So** I went and washed ... and **then** I could see."

"Is he **here**? Is he with **you**?"

"**Where** is this man? This **Jesus**?"

"I ... do **not** know."

33

THEY DIDN'T BELIEVE HIM.
WHAT'S THAT?
THE BEGGAR. THE PEOPLE DIDN'T BELIEVE WHAT HE WAS TELLING THEM ABOUT THE MIRACLE.
EVEN THOUGH THE EVIDENCE WAS PLAIN, THEY DIDN'T BELIEVE A BLIND MAN COULD SUDDENLY SEE.
CORRECT. THEY WERE AS UNSEEING AS THE POOR BEGGAR HAD BEEN BEFORE HIS VISION WAS RESTORED.
SO WHAT DOES THAT SAY OF US?
OF ALL MANKIND?
TO TRUST WHAT IS IN FRONT OF OUR VERY EYES?
THAT DOESN'T HELP ME. I'VE BEEN BLIND AS LONG AS I CAN REMEMBER.
NO, NO. I MEAN SPIRITUAL VISION! WE MUST LEARN TO ACCEPT WHAT GOD PRESENTS TO US. WE MUST HAVE FAITH.
THE PEOPLE TOOK THE BEGGAR, AS WELL AS HIS PARENTS, TO THE PHARISEES* IN AN ATTEMPT TO VERIFY THE OBVIOUS MIRACLE THAT HAD OCCURRED.
AS YOU MIGHT IMAGINE, THIS VISIT DID NOT GO WELL.
*PHARISEES: STRICT OBSERVERS OF JEWISH RITES AND CEREMONIES INVOLVING RELIGION, HISTORY, AND WRITTEN LAW.

"**NOW** THE DAY ON WHICH JESUS HAD **OPENED** THE MAN'S **EYES** WAS A **SABBATH**."

This man who placed the mud on your eyes is **not** from **God**, for he does not keep the **Sabbath**, which is a **sin!**

How can a man who is a sinner perform such **miraculous signs?**

What say you about this **Jesus?** It was your eyes he **opened.**

He is a **prophet.**

We **know** this is our son, and we know he **was born blind.**

We **do not** know how it is that he **now sees,** nor do we know who **opened** his eyes.

Ask **our son.** He is of age. He will speak for **himself.**

Give glory to God. We **know** that this man who touched you is a **sinner.**

"HIS **PARENTS** SAID THIS BECAUSE THEY **WERE AFRAID,** FOR THE JEWS HAD DECIDED THAT **ANYONE** WHO CONFESSED **JESUS** TO BE THE MESSIAH WOULD BE PUT OUT OF THE **SYNAGOGUE**."

I **do not** know whether he is a sinner. **One** thing I do know. Though I was **blind,** now I see.

35

So what did he do to you?
How did he open your eyes?
I have told you already, and you did not listen. Why do you want to hear it again?
Do you want to become his disciples, too?
You can be his disciple, but we are disciples of Moses!
We know that God has spoken to Moses, but as for this man, we don't even know where he comes from!
His home is of no consequence, don't you see?
He has healed my blindness!
Not since the world began has anyone opened the eyes of a man born blind.
If this man was not from God, he couldn't perform miracles in God's name.
Silence! We have heard enough!
You, who were steeped in sin at birth, dare lecture us?
You dare?!

SO, THE BEGGAR COULD SEE, RIGHT? BLIND FROM BIRTH, BUT BLIND NO MORE.
CORRECT.
GIVING A BLIND MAN SIGHT IS A MIRACLE, PLAIN AND TRUE!
WELL. THEY THREW THE BEGGAR AND HIS PARENTS OUT ONTO THE STREET.
DIDN'T THEY WANT TO KNOW HOW HE WAS ABLE TO SEE?
YES.
SO, WHAT DID THE PHARISEES DO THEN?
WANTING TO KNOW THE TRUTH IS ONE THING. AND BELIEVING WHAT ONE IS TOLD IS TRUE IS ANOTHER.
THEY COULD NOT ACCEPT THAT JESUS WAS CAPABLE OF SUCH WORKS, SO THEY CALLED THE BEGGAR A LIAR.
WHAT HAPPENED AFTER THAT?
JESUS HEARD THAT THE PHARISEES REJECTED THE TALE OF THE MAN HE HAD HEALED, SO HE CAME BACK TO VISIT WITH THE BEGGAR A FINAL TIME.

Do you believe in the Son of Man?
And who is he, sir? Tell me, so that I may believe in him.
You have now seen him, for he is the one speaking with you.
Lord, I believe.
For judgment I have come into this world, so that those who are blind -- both physically and spiritually -- will see.

"What do you **mean** by those **words**?"

"Surely we are not blind!"

"**Ask** the Father to open the **eyes** of **your heart** that you may see clearly. Then you **will truly** know **what** it means to have **vision**."

"SO IT **WAS** THAT JESUS **HEALED** A SINGLE **BLIND** MAN AND **YET** WAS ABLE TO REACH MANY MORE SOULS WHO ALSO **SUFFERED** FROM A **LACK** OF SPIRITUAL VISION."

"SO THERE WERE **OTHER PEOPLE** BESIDES THE BEGGAR WHO **COULDN'T SEE**?"

"OH, THEY **COULD SEE** WITH THEIR EYES, BUT THEY **WERE BLIND** ON THE INSIDE TO THE GLORIES OF **GOD'S TEACHINGS** AND TO THE PRESENCE OF **HIS SON** IN THEIR VERY **MIDST**."

AVA, HOW LONG HAVE YOU BEEN WITHOUT SIGHT?
I WAS BORN THIS WAY.
BORN BLIND, YET YOU SEE SO MUCH. THE WORLD IS OPEN TO YOUR EYES, CHILD.
AND UNLIKE THE PHARISEES I TOLD YOU ABOUT, YOU DO NOT SUFFER FROM A LACK OF SPIRITUAL VISION OR OF FAITH.
I ASKED YOU EARLIER IF YOU BELIEVED IN MIRACLES. DO YOU, AVA?
YES.
AND DO YOU HAVE FAITH IN THE LORD AND HIS PLAN FOR ALL OF US HERE ON EARTH?
I DO.
I WANT YOU TO CLOSE YOUR EYES.
WHY? IT MAKES NO DIFFERENCE WHETHER I --
JUST CLOSE THEM AND PERHAPS --
JUST PERHAPS --

-- THIS TIME, WHEN YOU OPEN THEM, YOU WILL SEE A DIFFERENCE.
RAINFREDIS?
RAINFREDIS, WHERE DID YOU GO?
OH.
I CAN SEE!
IT'S A MIRACLE!
41

THANK YOU, LORD.
THANK YOU!
RAINFREDIS! I UNDERSTAND, NOW!
I UNDERSTAND WHAT YOU WERE TELLING ME!
RAINFREDIS? WHERE ARE YOU?
I UNDERSTAND -- OHH!
I KNOW THIS GARDEN INCH BY INCH, EACH AND EVERY PLANT.
AND NOW THAT I CAN SEE, I FALL WITH MY FIRST STEP!
AVA! YOU MUST BE MORE CAREFUL!
WHERE IS HE? WHERE DID HE GO?
WHO, AVA?
RAINFREDIS! HE WAS RIGHT HERE WITH ME!

"RAINFREDIS? AVA, THERE IS NO VISITOR HERE BY THAT NAME.

I WAS WATCHING YOU FROM THE CASTLE--

YOU'VE BEEN ALONE ALL AFTERNOON."

JUST AS IN THE CASE OF THIS HUMBLE BLIND MAN IN THE GOSPEL, EVERYONE WILL BE SHOWN THE LIGHT. THOSE WHO ARE HUMBLE WILL SEE AND ACCEPT GOD, AND THE PROUD WILL BE BLINDED IN THEIR ARROGANCE.

43

AVA **CONTINUED** TO SERVE **THE LORD** WITH HER LIFE. SHE CONSIDERED THE MIRACULOUS GIFT OF **SIGHT** A **TREASURE**, NEVER TO BE TAKEN FOR **GRANTED**.

AFTER **GROWING** INTO ADULTHOOD, SHE LEFT THE CASTLE AND **ENTERED** A **CONVENT** AT DINART, HAINAULT.

SOON **AFTERWARDS**, IN RECOGNITION OF HER PIETY AND **EFFORTS**, SHE WAS **ELECTED** AS ABBESS.

AFTER THAT **DAY** IN THE GARDEN, AVA WAS NEVER TO HEAR OF **RAINFREDIS AGAIN**.

YET, SHE **NEVER FORGOT** THE LESSON HE SHARED, NOR THE **GIFT** HE HELPED **BESTOW**.

IT WAS **HERE** SHE BECAME A **BENEDICTINE NUN**.

THE END.

HINDSIGHT
The Life of St. Ava

The dates surrounding the **life** of St. Ava are obscure. We do know that she lived in the castle during the reign of **King Pepin**, and by using the dates of his **marriage** as a **guide**, would place St. Ava's birth sometime between **740** and **760**.

Though she was born **blind**, and later **miraculously cured**, her actions after this event are why she is **remembered** today.

Stunned by the **beauty** of the world and thankful to God for **granting** her the **gift of sight**, St. Ava devoted her life to the service of the **Lord**. She entered a convent at **Dinart**, Hainault and became a **Benedictine Nun**. So **great** was her **piety** that she was elected as **abbess**, and she stayed in this role until **her death**.

Her **feast** day is **April 29th**.

Have you ever been misunderstood?

SAINT SAMSON

SAINT SAMSON

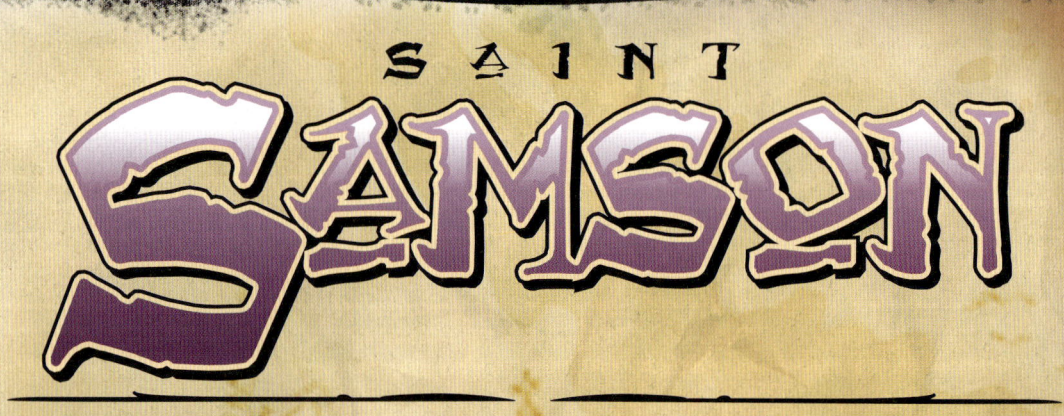

Once Upon a Time...

The life of **St. Samson** is well documented. Since his death of old age in **565**, his story has captivated those seeking **guidance** in the pursuit of their faith. A private man who spent **many years** as a hermit, Samson **preferred** the solitude of his **own company**... yet never hesitated to respond when called to **serve the Lord**.

His history, like many saints of his times, varies. Some **legends** tell of St. Samson **locked** in a battle to the death with a **fearsome dragon**. **Others** have him in several places at the same time, as he traveled **throughout Europe** carrying out his missionary work. Regardless of these accounts, **one thing** is certain -- St. Samson **never wavered** in his faith in God and was richly rewarded with a **long life**. He spent his days with members of his loving family at his side, **helping his fellow man**.

St. Samson **died** around the **age of 80** years old, in peace, and was buried on the grounds of his **beloved monastery** in **Dol**.

PRODUCER: Daniel Burton

EDITORIAL: Kimberly Black

STORY: Terry Collins

ART: Jason Millet

LETTERS / DESIGNS: Keith Bahrenburg

ONCE UPON A TIME IN WEST WALES, THERE WAS A *MONSTROUS* DRAGON *TERRORIZING* THE LAND ...

A MAGICAL CREATURE, THE DRAGON POSSESSED A BREATH OF PURE FIRE THAT WAS DEADLY TO ANY LIVING BEING --

-- WHETHER MAN OR BEAST.

THE DRAGON HAD BEEN ON A RAMPAGE --

-- DESTROYING VILLAGES ACROSS THE LAND.

THE PEOPLE OF WALES WERE TERRIFIED FOR THEIR LIVES, AND PRAYED FOR A HERO TO SAVE THEM.

THAT HERO WAS THE MIGHTY BISHOP SAMSON --

-- WHO BROUGHT A STRONG RIGHT ARM TO WIELD HIS BLADE --

-- AND THE POWER OF THE LORD AT HIS BACK.

SAMSON LEARNED FROM THE VILLAGERS *THE CREATURE* LIVED IN A DARK CAVE NEAR THE COAST, *HIGH ABOVE* THE SEA.

RATHER THAN WAIT FOR *ANOTHER ATTACK*, HE TOOK THE BATTLE DIRECTLY TO THE *DRAGON'S LAIR*.

THE *WARRIOR* FOUGHT LONG AND HARD, BUT MAN AND CREATURE SEEMED TO BE *EVENLY MATCHED*, WITH *NEITHER* MAKING HEADWAY.

AND THEN, *BRAVE SAMSON ABANDONED* HIS SWORD AND DECIDED TO USE HIS *BARE HANDS!*

THE *MANUEVER* WAS SUCCESSFUL. THE DRAGON *TOPPLED* OVER THE *EDGE* OF THE CLIFF AND TUMBLED TO A *WATERY DOOM*.

51

560 A.D. THE DIOCESE OF DOL, LOCATED IN NORTH BRITTANY.
SO YOU SEE, AFTER HEARING SUCH TALES ... WE WERE HONORED WHEN YOU AGREED TO MEET WITH US TODAY, BISHOP SAMSON!
YOUR DEEDS ARE AN INSPIRATION TO US ALL. YOU'RE A LIVING LEGEND!
YOUR STORY IS ONE OF HOPE AND FAITH! LIFE AND DEATH! HEAVEN AND HELL!
GENTLEMEN...
SURELY YOU JEST!

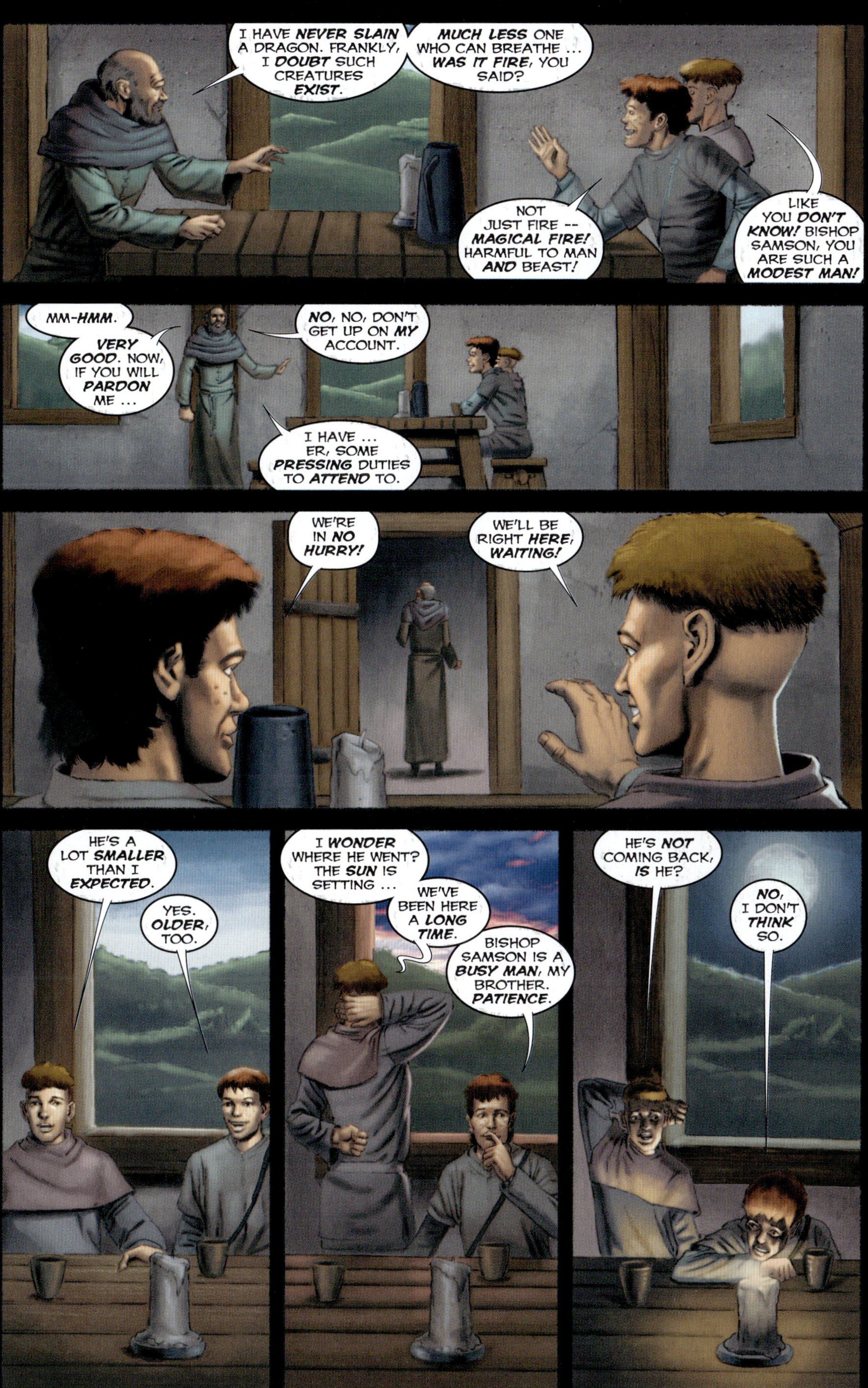
I HAVE NEVER SLAIN A DRAGON. FRANKLY, I DOUBT SUCH CREATURES EXIST.
MUCH LESS ONE WHO CAN BREATHE ... WAS IT FIRE, YOU SAID?
NOT JUST FIRE -- MAGICAL FIRE! HARMFUL TO MAN AND BEAST!
LIKE YOU DON'T KNOW! BISHOP SAMSON, YOU ARE SUCH A MODEST MAN!
MM-HMM.
VERY GOOD. NOW, IF YOU WILL PARDON ME ...
NO, NO, DON'T GET UP ON MY ACCOUNT.
I HAVE ... ER, SOME PRESSING DUTIES TO ATTEND TO.
WE'RE IN NO HURRY!
WE'LL BE RIGHT HERE, WAITING!
HE'S A LOT SMALLER THAN I EXPECTED.
YES. OLDER, TOO.
I WONDER WHERE HE WENT? THE SUN IS SETTING ...
WE'VE BEEN HERE A LONG TIME.
BISHOP SAMSON IS A BUSY MAN, MY BROTHER. PATIENCE.
HE'S NOT COMING BACK, IS HE?
NO, I DON'T THINK SO.

WHERE IS EVERYONE?
DO YOU THINK THEY ARE SLEEPING?
THE HOUR ISN'T THAT LATE ... BUT I CONFESS I'VE LOST TRACK OF TIME.
I GUESS THE SAME THING HAPPENED TO THE BISHOP -- THAT'S WHY HE NEVER RETURNED.
HE PROBABLY HAS TRAVELERS LIKE US ARRIVING DAILY, WANTING TO TALK.
I GUESS WE DIDN'T DO SUCH A GOOD JOB OF GRABBING HIS ATTENTION.
MAY I OFFER ASSISTANCE?
GAHHHH!
AIIEE!
OH, YOU ARE BISHOP SAMSON'S VISITORS. WE THOUGHT YOU HAD LEFT.
NO, NOT YET. WE STILL HAVE QUESTIONS.

THIS IS OUR LIBRARY. A GOOD PLACE TO HAVE QUESTIONS ANSWERED. WHAT KNOWLEDGE DO YOU SEEK?
WE TRAVELED HUNDREDS OF MILES TO LEARN MORE OF THE GREATNESS OF BISHOP SAMSON, WORKER OF MIRACLES, SLAYER OF DRAGONS.
WILL HE BE JOINING US?
UM, NO ...
NOT LIKELY. HOWEVER, I AM WELL VERSED IN HIS HISTORY.
YOU WILL UNDOUBTEDLY LEARN MORE FROM MY LIPS THAN HIS -- THE BISHOP DOES NOT ENJOY TALKING ABOUT HIS MANY ACCOMPLISHMENTS.
WHERE WOULD YOU LIKE ME TO START?
HOW ABOUT AT THE BEGINNING?
THE BEGINNING IT SHALL BE.
BISHOP SAMSON WAS BORN ABOUT THE YEAR 485.
HIS FATHER, AMON, WAS OF THE WELSH PROVINCE OF DYFED; HIS MOTHER, ANNA, A LADY OF GWENT.

SAMSON'S *BIRTH* WAS CONSIDERED A *BLESSING*, SINCE HIS PARENTS HAD BEEN CHILDLESS FOR *MANY YEARS*.

TO *CELEBRATE* THIS GIFT OF A SON, HIS FATHER DEDICATED THE BOY *TO GOD*.

AT THE *AGE OF FIVE*, HE BEGAN HIS STUDIES IN THE *MONASTERY* FOUNDED AND GOVERNED BY *ST. ILLTUD* AT LLANTWIT IN GLAMORGAN.

THE *YOUNG* SAMSON WAS MOST *VIRTUOUS* IN HIS LIFE --

DEDICATED *WITHOUT FAIL* TO LIVING SIMPLY AND *HUMBLY* AS A MONK, HIS *TALENTS* DID NOT GO UNNOTICED.

-- SPENDING HIS *TIME* IN RESEARCH AND *THOUGHT*.

HE WAS *QUICK* IN HIS STUDIES, BRINGING *NEW EYES* TO THE ANCIENT *TEXTS*.

AS A SERVANT TO GOD HE WAS REWARDED --

-- BY ARCHBISHOP DUBRICIUS, WHO MADE SAMSON A DEACON AND PRIEST.

SOON AFTER, SAMSON WAS CALLED TO A SMALL ISLAND OFF THE COAST OF PEMBROKESHIRE TO OFFER RELIGIOUS GUIDANCE AND COUNSEL.

NEVER ONE FOR TRAVELING, THIS WAS LUCKILY A SHORT TRIP.

SAMSON HAD NOT BEEN IN RESIDENCE LONG WHEN A MESSAGE CAME FROM HIS MOTHER. AMON, HIS FATHER, WAS DYING, AND SHE HAD SENT FOR HER SON.

I LOVE MY FATHER, GOVERNOR PIRO --

BUT ANOTHER OF GOD'S SERVANTS CAN ADMINISTER THE LAST RITES. MY PLACE IS HERE.

THE GOVERNOR DISAGREED, AND REBUKED SAMSON ... SENDING HIM ACROSS THE WATER TO HIS FATHER'S DEATHBED.

UPON *ARRIVAL*, SAMSON WAS TOLD HIS FATHER *DID NOT* HAVE LONG TO *LIVE*.

HE *ENTERED* THE BEDROOM AND *ADMINISTERED* THE SACRAMENTS.

LATER, AMON WAS TO *SAY* THAT WHEN HE LOOKED UP AT *HIS SON*, ALL HE COULD SEE WAS A VIBRANT *WHITE LIGHT*.

AMON *BELIEVED* HE WAS BOUND FOR THE KINGDOM OF *HEAVEN*, BUT INSTEAD --

-- RECOVERED *ALMOST INSTANTLY* FROM HIS ILLNESS.

AS WORD *SPREAD* OF AMON'S *RECOVERY* AT THE HANDS OF HIS SON, OTHERS CAME TO *BEAR WITNESS*.

SAMSON, *MY SON*, LET ME JOIN YOU IN YOUR *HOLY WORK*. FOR SURELY I HAVE BEEN SAVED TO DO *GOOD THINGS*.

SAMSON *COULD NOT* STAY, SO HIS *FATHER* AND HIS UNCLE *UMBRAFEL* BOTH ACCOMPANIED HIM *BACK* TO THE ISLAND.

UPON HIS **RETURN**, HE DISCOVERED PIRO HAD DIED. SAMSON WAS MADE **ABBOT** IN HIS **STEAD**.

THE **DUTIES** OF THE OFFICE WEIGHED UPON HIS **MIND** --

-- ALLOWING **LITTLE TIME** FOR **INNER PEACE** AND REFLECTION.

HE MADE A **JOURNEY** TO **IRELAND** TO QUELL TROUBLE AT A MONASTERY, BUT **AGAIN** WAS **NOT HAPPY** TO BE SO FAR FROM HIS ADOPTED **HOMELAND**.

SAMSON LEFT HIS **UNCLE UMBRAFEL** IN CHARGE AND RETURNED TO THE **ISLAND**.

THIS **LAST TRIP** WAS ENOUGH FOR SAMSON, WHO **STEPPED DOWN** FROM HIS **POST** AS ABBOT AND **RETIRED**.

ALONG WITH HIS **LOYAL FATHER** AND **TWO OTHER** FOLLOWERS, HE SETTLED NEAR THE **RIVER SEVERN** AND BECAME A **HERMIT**.

I **DO NOT** QUESTION YOU, MY SON, BUT I WONDER IF **THIS LIFE** YOU HAVE NOW CHOSEN IS **THE BEST USE** OF YOUR ABILITIES.

FOR ME, IT IS THE **ONLY CHOICE**. FOR THE FIRST TIME IN YEARS I AM **AT PEACE**.

SADLY, HIS PEACE WAS TO BE SHORT LIVED.
WHY? WHAT HAPPENED NEXT?
WE KNOW HE DIDN'T STAY A HERMIT -- HE WAS JUST GETTING STARTED, RIGHT?
YES -- AND BISHOP SAMSON STILL HASN'T GONE TO THE CAVE TO FIGHT THE DRAGON EITHER!
RIGHT! IS THIS THE PART WHERE HE BECOMES A DRAGON SLAYER?
SIGH --
AGAIN WITH THE DRAGON ...
NO, WHAT HAPPENED WAS THIS. THE ARCHBISHOP AGAIN SUMMONED SAMSON AND THIS TIME CONSECRATED HIM AS BISHOP.
DESPITE SAMSON'S WISHES TO STAY HIDDEN AWAY, HE KNEW HE WAS CHOSEN. GOD HAD ANOTHER PLAN FOR HIS LOYAL SERVANT.
ON EASTER EVE, WHILE IN PRAYER, THE NEWLY-APPOINTED BISHOP HAD A VISION.

SAMSON, THIS IS NOT THE TIME FOR YOU TO REST.
THERE ARE MANY SEEDS TO BE PLANTED IN THE GARDENS OF THE WORLD.
YOU MUST BE THAT GARDENER AND TEND TO THE CROPS YET TO COME.
YOU HAVE A MISSION. YOUR FATE HAS YET TO BE FULFILLED.
ONE DAY YOU WILL RETURN TO THE PEACE YOU DESIRE, BUT NOT TODAY.
HE WAS TOLD TO LEAVE THE ISLAND AND GO BEYOND THE SEAS -- WHERE HE WOULD CONFRONT HIS DESTINY.

FOR MONTHS, HE TRAVELED ACROSS ENGLAND BY MEANS OF A CHARIOT HE HAD BOUGHT IN IRELAND.
WITH HIS FATHER BY HIS SIDE, THE BISHOP SPREAD THE WORD OF GOD TO ALL HE ENCOUNTERED.
ONE DAY WHILE TRAVELING THROUGH THE DISTRICT OF TRIGG, HE FOUND A GROUP OF PEOPLE IN CRISIS.
CAN THESE BE THE IDOL WORSHIPPERS WE WERE TOLD ABOUT?
STOP AND WE SHALL SEE.
MY SON WAS THROWN FROM HIS HORSE AND NOW LIES UNMOVING. I FEAR HE IS DEAD.
PERHAPS I CAN HELP.
I'VE HEARD OF THIS MAN. BISHOP SAMSON IS HIS NAME. THEY SAY HIS GOD IS THE ONE GOD AND CAN WORK MIRACLES.
GAH!
THE STORIES ARE TRUE!

IN MERE **MOMENTS**, A LIFE WAS **RESTORED**, AND THE SOULS OF THE ENTIRE VILLAGE **WERE SAVED**.

AFTER **BISHOP SAMSON** LEFT, REST ASSURED ANY **FALSE IDOLS** WERE **CAST AWAY** FOR THE **LORD**.

HE FOUNDED A **CHURCH** AT **SOUTHILL**, LEAVING HIS FATHER IN CHARGE OF **THE MONASTERY**.

ANOTHER CHURCH, ONE OF DOZENS IN HIS WAKE, WAS **BUILT SOON** AFTER AT **GOLANT**.

NOW **ALONE** IN HIS **JOURNEY**, SAMSON TOOK A SHIP TO **BRITTANY**.

FROM **HERE**, HE WAS TO KEEP MAKING HIS **MISSIONARY TRIPS** IN **ALL DIRECTIONS** OF THE WORLD.

HE **HELPED** TO RESTORE TO BRITTANY ITS **RIGHTFUL PRINCE**, JUDUAL.

AND WHILE **VISITING PARIS**, HE ATTRACTED THE NOTICE OF **KING CHILDEBERT**, WHO NOMINATED SAMSON AS **BISHOP OF DOL**.

FINALLY, HE FOUNDED TWO MONASTERIES: ONE AT PENTAL IN NORMANDY, AND THE SECOND ONE RIGHT HERE IN DOL.

NOW IN ADVANCED AGE, THE BISHOP HAS RETURNED TO THE SECLUSION HE HAS ALWAYS CRAVED, LIVING HAPPILY AMONGST US HERE IN QUIET STUDY.

AND *THAT'S IT?* NO DRAGONS?

WEREN'T YOU LISTENING? *BISHOP SAMSON* HAS DINED WITH *KINGS* AND WORKED *MIRACLES* --

WHO *CARES* ABOUT A *SILLY OLD DRAGON?*

WHO'S IN HERE? THE HOUR IS MUCH *TOO LATE* FOR STUDY, EVEN ON A *SLEEPLESS NIGHT*.

OH. *YOU TWO*. KEEPING UP *THE MONKS*, ARE WE?

NOT AT ALL, BISHOP SAMSON. I WAS *CORRECTING* THEM REGARDING YOUR LIFE AND *DEEDS*.

MY LIFE IS ONE OF SERVICE, NOT ONE TO BE *BRAGGED* ABOUT TO *VISITORS!*

I SPOKE ONLY *THE TRUTH*, BISHOP. *THEY* ARE THE ONES IN SEARCH OF *A CHAMPION*.

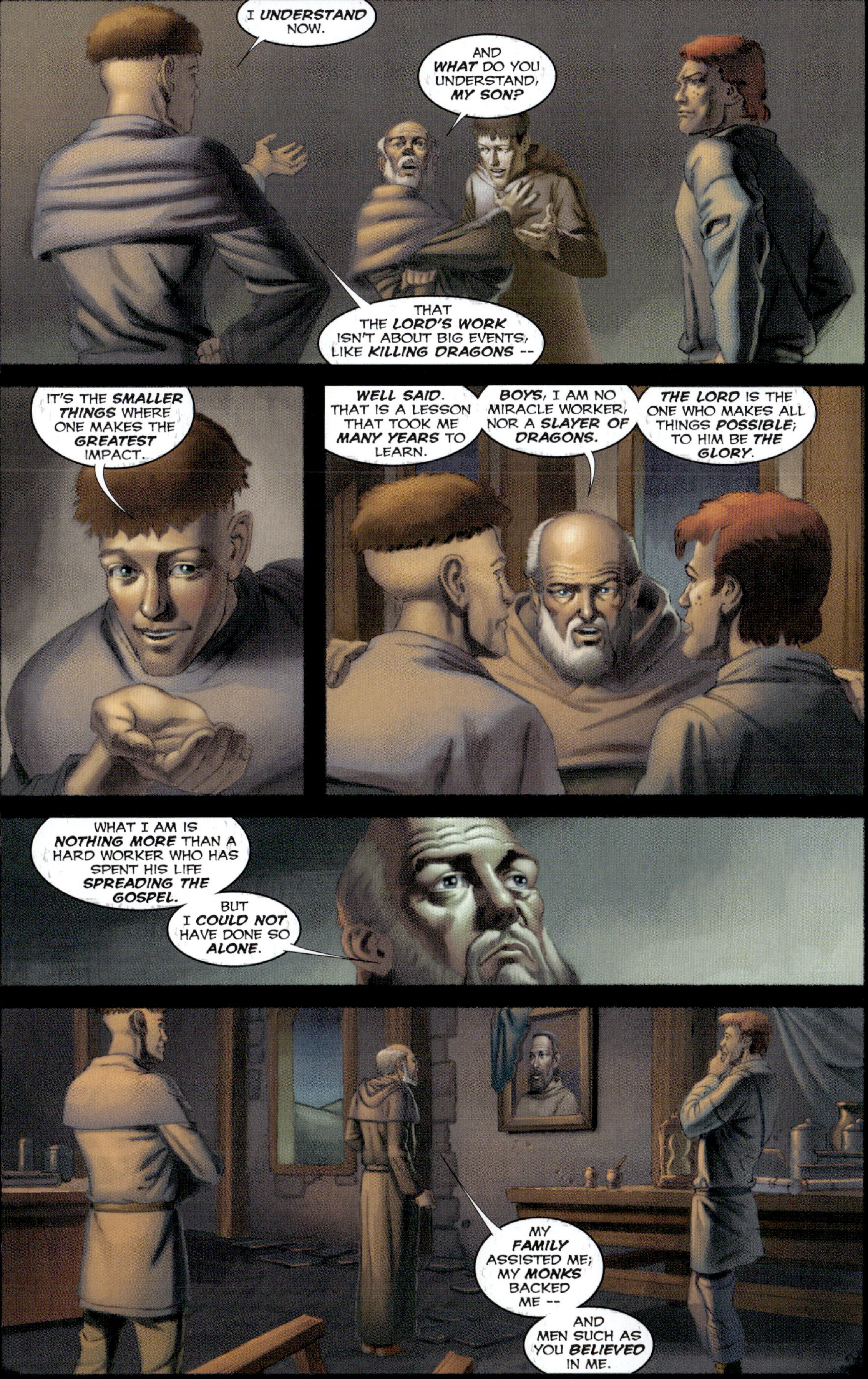
I UNDERSTAND NOW.
AND WHAT DO YOU UNDERSTAND, MY SON?
THAT THE LORD'S WORK ISN'T ABOUT BIG EVENTS, LIKE KILLING DRAGONS --
IT'S THE SMALLER THINGS WHERE ONE MAKES THE GREATEST IMPACT.
WELL SAID. THAT IS A LESSON THAT TOOK ME MANY YEARS TO LEARN.
BOYS, I AM NO MIRACLE WORKER, NOR A SLAYER OF DRAGONS.
THE LORD IS THE ONE WHO MAKES ALL THINGS POSSIBLE; TO HIM BE THE GLORY.
WHAT I AM IS NOTHING MORE THAN A HARD WORKER WHO HAS SPENT HIS LIFE SPREADING THE GOSPEL.
BUT I COULD NOT HAVE DONE SO ALONE.
MY FAMILY ASSISTED ME; MY MONKS BACKED ME --
AND MEN SUCH AS YOU BELIEVED IN ME.

INSTEAD OF AVOIDING YOUR QUESTIONS, I SHOULD HAVE WELCOMED THEM --
FOR THE TRUTH ONLY APPEARS WHEN KNOWLEDGE IS SOUGHT OUT.
SO, THERE REALLY NEVER WAS A DRAGON?
ACTUALLY IT WAS A SERPENT.
A GIANT SERPENT?
QUITE LARGE, YES.
AS BIG AS A MAN?
WELL, IT WAS AS LONG AS A MAN IS TALL, AND JUST AS QUICK.
DID IT HAVE WINGS?
BREATHE FIRE?
NO, NO. JUST A SERPENT. NO FLYING, NO FIRE. THE KING WAS HAPPY WHEN I KILLED THE CREATURE AND THREW IT INTO THE SEA.
BISHOP, WE CAME SEEKING A HERO. WE HAVE FOUND THAT MAN.
WE WOULD BE HONORED TO ASSIST YOU IN YOUR WORK. IF YOU WOULD HAVE US.
THEN, RISE. WE CAN DISCUSS YOUR ROLES HERE AT THE MONASTERY IN THE MORNING.
FOR NOW, LET US SLEEP --
KNOWING WE ARE ALL SAFE WITHIN THESE WALLS, AND IN GOD'S HANDS.

A Look At A Legend

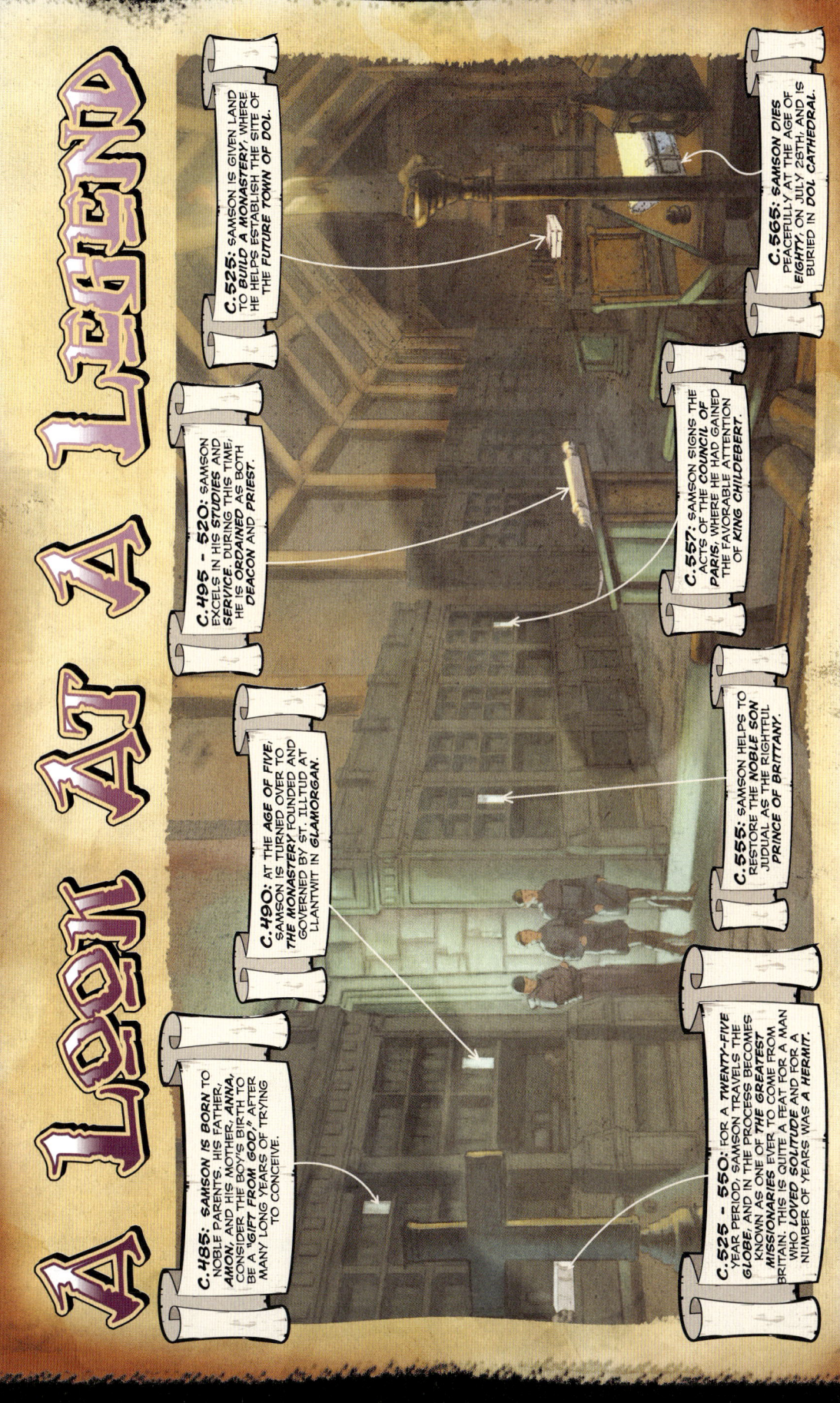

C.485: SAMSON IS BORN TO NOBLE PARENTS, HIS FATHER, AMON, AND HIS MOTHER, ANNA, CONSIDER THE BOY'S BIRTH TO BE A *"GIFT FROM GOD,"* AFTER MANY LONG YEARS OF TRYING TO CONCEIVE.

C.490: AT THE AGE OF FIVE, SAMSON IS TURNED OVER TO *THE MONASTERY* FOUNDED AND GOVERNED BY ST. ILLTUD AT LLANTWIT IN *GLAMORGAN*.

C.495 - 520: SAMSON EXCELS IN HIS *STUDIES* AND *SERVICE*. DURING THIS TIME, HE IS ORDAINED AS BOTH *DEACON AND PRIEST*.

C.525: SAMSON IS GIVEN LAND TO *BUILD A MONASTERY*, WHERE HE HELPS ESTABLISH THE SITE OF THE *FUTURE TOWN OF DOL*.

C.525 - 550: FOR A *TWENTY-FIVE* YEAR PERIOD, SAMSON TRAVELS THE *GLOBE*, AND IN THE PROCESS BECOMES KNOWN AS ONE OF *THE GREATEST MISSIONARIES* EVER TO COME FROM BRITAIN. THIS IS QUITE A FEAT FOR A MAN WHO *LOVED SOLITUDE* AND FOR A NUMBER OF YEARS WAS A *HERMIT*.

C.555: SAMSON HELPS TO RESTORE THE *NOBLE SON* JUDUAL AS THE RIGHTFUL *PRINCE OF BRITTANY*.

C.557: SAMSON SIGNS THE ACTS OF THE *COUNCIL OF PARIS*, WHERE HE HAD GAINED THE FAVORABLE ATTENTION OF *KING CHILDEBERT*.

C.565: *SAMSON DIES PEACEFULLY AT THE AGE OF EIGHTY*, ON JULY 28TH, AND IS BURIED IN *DOL CATHEDRAL*.

How do you react when someone doesn't believe you?

Saint Bernadette

Saint Bernadette

The Saint of Lourdes, France
AUTHORED BY JEN MURVIN EDWARDS

IMAGINE A YOUNG GIRL. SHE'S SMALL FOR HER AGE, **QUIET** AND **SICKLY**. SHE'S NOT ABLE TO ATTEND SCHOOL -- **NO**, SHE IS SICK **TOO OFTEN** -- AND MANY TIMES MUST STAY IN BED FOR DAYS TO RECUPERATE. HER **FIVE** BROTHERS AND **SISTERS** KEEP HER WELL-ENTERTAINED, BUT IN TIMES OF QUIET AND **SOLITUDE**, SHE DOUBTS HER INTELLECT AND VALUE. SHE IS AN UNASSUMING CHILD WHO FINDS **HOPE AND PEACE** IN THE ONE BOOK SHE IS ABLE TO KNOW: **THE BIBLE**.

BERNADETTE IN HER YOUTH
IMAGES BY RON LIM
COLORS BY DANIEL BURTON

ST. BERNADETTE, THE BELOVED **SAINT OF LOURDES, FRANCE**, WAS THE **VERY CHILD** DESCRIBED ABOVE. HER **HUMBLE** UPBRINGING **SERVED** TO PROVIDE YOUNG BERNADETTE WITH THE TOOLS SHE WOULD USE TO **BRING THE MESSAGE** OF **OUR LADY** TO ALL OF FRANCE AND, LATER, THE WORLD: A **MODEST ATTITUDE, UNWAVERING FAITH**, AND **UNQUESTIONABLE SPIRIT**.

ST. BERNADETTE'S **VISIONS** OF OUR LADY AND THE **MIRACLES OF THE LOURDES SPRING** HAVE REMAINED IN THE **HEART** AND **HISTORY** OF FRANCE FOR **CENTURIES**. AS A **RESULT** OF HER MANY VISIONS, BERNADETTE WAS **REPEATEDLY HARASSED** BY BOTH **ENEMIES** AND **ADMIRERS**, AND THUS WAS COMPELLED AT THE AGE OF TWENTY-TWO TO ENTER THE **SISTERS OF NOTRE DAME AT NEVERS**. THERE SHE SPENT THE **REST** OF HER YEARS UNTIL HER DEATH IN 1879 AT THE AGE OF **THIRTY-FIVE**. IT IS SAID THAT **HER SOUL** WAS **SO INNOCENT** THAT HER BODY DEFIED THE **LAWS OF NATURE** AND REMAINED INTACT IN HER COFFIN FOR **OVER A CENTURY**.

PRODUCED BY DANIEL BURTON   EDITORIALS BY KIMBERLY BLACK   TYPOGRAPHIC DESIGNS BY KEITH BAHRENBURG

LOURDES, FRANCE. 1858.
WE SHOULD GO HOME, BERNADETTE --
YOU'VE ONLY JUST BECOME WELL AGAIN!
MOTHER WILL BE SO ANGRY IF SHE LEARNS WE'VE VENTURED THIS FAR FROM HOME.
JUST A BIT FARTHER! IT'S BEEN SO LONG SINCE MY EYES HAVE GAZED UPON ANYTHING BUT THE BLANKETS ON MY BED AND THE COBWEBS ON THE CEILING.
WELL ... WHEN YOU PUT IT THAT WAY, I CANNOT PROTEST.
OF COURSE NOT --
FOR HOW COULD YOU REFUSE YOUR POOR SISTER THE SUNLIGHT SHE HAS BEEN DENIED SO LONG?
BUT YOU ARE RIGHT, THE HOUR GROWS LATE.
THEN, PLEASE, I WILL BEG ONCE MORE. LET US RETURN HOME --
THE JOURNEY BACK WILL SURELY BE LONG ENOUGH TO SATISFY EVEN YOUR DEPRIVED SPIRIT!

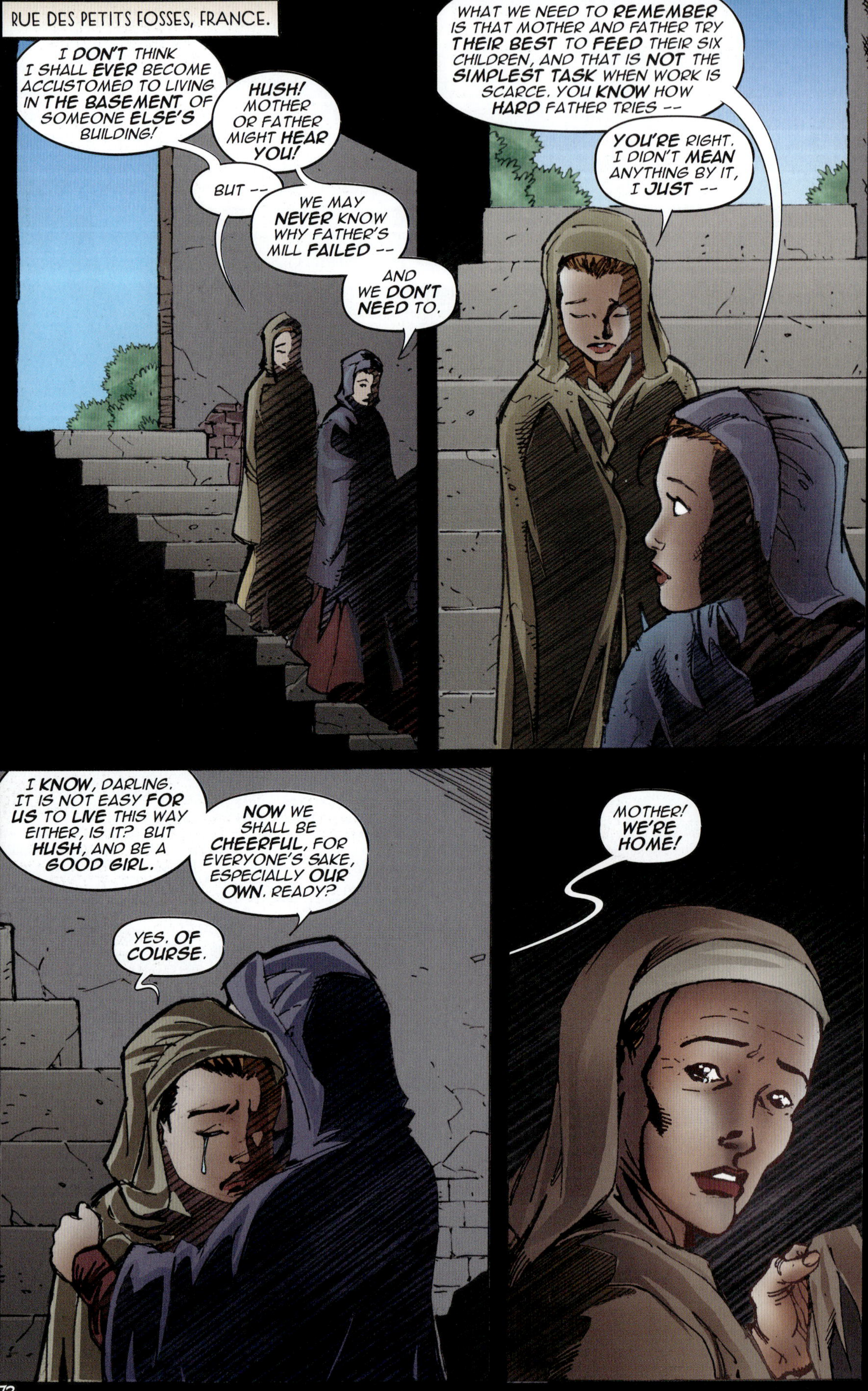
RUE DES PETITS FOSSES, FRANCE.
I DON'T THINK I SHALL EVER BECOME ACCUSTOMED TO LIVING IN THE BASEMENT OF SOMEONE ELSE'S BUILDING!
HUSH! MOTHER OR FATHER MIGHT HEAR YOU!
BUT --
WE MAY NEVER KNOW WHY FATHER'S MILL FAILED --
AND WE DON'T NEED TO.
WHAT WE NEED TO REMEMBER IS THAT MOTHER AND FATHER TRY THEIR BEST TO FEED THEIR SIX CHILDREN, AND THAT IS NOT THE SIMPLEST TASK WHEN WORK IS SCARCE. YOU KNOW HOW HARD FATHER TRIES --
YOU'RE RIGHT. I DIDN'T MEAN ANYTHING BY IT, I JUST --
I KNOW, DARLING. IT IS NOT EASY FOR US TO LIVE THIS WAY EITHER, IS IT? BUT HUSH, AND BE A GOOD GIRL.
NOW WE SHALL BE CHEERFUL, FOR EVERYONE'S SAKE, ESPECIALLY OUR OWN. READY?
YES. OF COURSE.
MOTHER! WE'RE HOME!

LATER THAT NIGHT...

I'VE BEEN **WAITING** TO SPEAK WITH YOU, **FRANCOIS.** TODAY I OVERHEARD THE **GIRLS** TALKING ON THE **STAIRS** AND --

PLEASE -- **NOT TONIGHT,** MY LOVE.

WE **CANNOT** KEEP AVOIDING THIS **CONVERSATION** -- YOU CANNOT **IGNORE** ALL OF THIS --

IGNORE THIS?! IGNORE THE FACT THAT MY FAMILY **EATS** AND **SLEEPS** IN THE BASEMENT OF **ANOTHER MAN'S DWELLING?!**

IT TAKES **EVERY OUNCE** OF MY **STRENGTH** TO EVEN **RISE** FROM MY **SLUMBER** EACH MORNING ...

FOR HOW MUCH **BETTER** IS IT TO LIVE **IN DREAMS,** WHERE I FEED MY WIFE AND FAMILY **CREAMS** AND **MEATS** AND LAY THEM DOWN ON BEDS OF **FEATHERS** ...

INSTEAD OF **THIS,** WHERE **BEDS** LINE THE FLOORS OF **A BASEMENT** AND MY CHILDREN FEED ON **SCRAPS** FROM BENEVOLENT MEN WHO SEE ME AS THE **FAILURE** I AM?

YOU ARE **NOT A FAILURE,** MY HUSBAND. IT'S JUST THAT **EVERY DAY** I LOOK AT BERNADETTE --

HER HEART **SO KIND,** BUT HER BODY TOO **SICKLY** TO ATTEND SCHOOL, **TOO WEAK** TO EVEN RECEIVE HER FIRST **COMMUNION!** SHE IS AN EXAMPLE TO US **ALL** ...

SHAME **ON ME,** HUSBAND, FOR **BLAMING** YOU WHEN I AM **THE ONE** WHO FEELS **SUCH GUILT** IN MY HEART.

73

THE NEXT MORNING. FEBRUARY 11, 1858.

BUT YOU WENT OUT *YESTERDAY*, BERNADETTE --

AND I *SURVIVED*, MOTHER. PLEASE, I WILL *NOT BE* LONG.

BUT IT IS GROWING *COLDER* --

ALL THE *MORE REASON*. I MUST COLLECT FIREWOOD TO KEEP US *ALL WARM!* PLEASE, MAY I?

YOUR SMILE IS *FAR TOO* PERSUASIVE, MY DAUGHTER.

ALRIGHT, YOU MAY GO, BUT *WRAP WARMLY* --

OF *COURSE*, MOTHER! I'LL *RETURN SOON!*

FINALLY! ALONE AT *LAST!*

THANK YOU, GOD, FOR *THIS* GIFT.

I DO *LOVE* MY BROTHERS AND SISTERS, OF *COURSE*. BUT YOU CAN'T FAULT A GIRL FOR WANTING SOME *TIME ALONE*, CAN YOU, FATHER?

SURELY THESE FLOWERS WILL **CHEER THE DARKNESS** OF THE BASEMENT.

PERHAPS THEY WILL ALSO MEND **MY HEART**. IF MOTHER AND FATHER KNEW JUST HOW **LIGHTLY I SLEEP**, THEY WOULD BE **MORE CAREFUL** WHEN **SPEAKING** AT NIGHT.

THEY MUST **NEVER REALIZE** I HEARD THEIR CONVERSATION -- EVEN FOR THE **SMALL TIME** BEFORE I WAS ABLE TO PUT **THE BLANKETS** OVER MY EARS TO **MUFFLE THEIR WORDS.**

EVEN THOUGH I AM A **SIMPLE GIRL**, I KNOW FOR CERTAIN **ONE THING**: GOD IS WATCHING **OVER ME**.

MY **BODY** SUFFERS, BUT MY **SPIRIT DOES NOT.**

ENOUGH OF THESE **IDLE MUSINGS**. IT'S TIME TO FIND SOME FIREWOOD. **SURELY I CAN ACCOMPLISH** THIS **SIMPLE TASK!**

OH MY! A GLOW ...

WHAT IS **THAT LIGHT?** I MUST DISCOVER ITS SOURCE; IT IS **SO BEAUTIFUL** ...

!

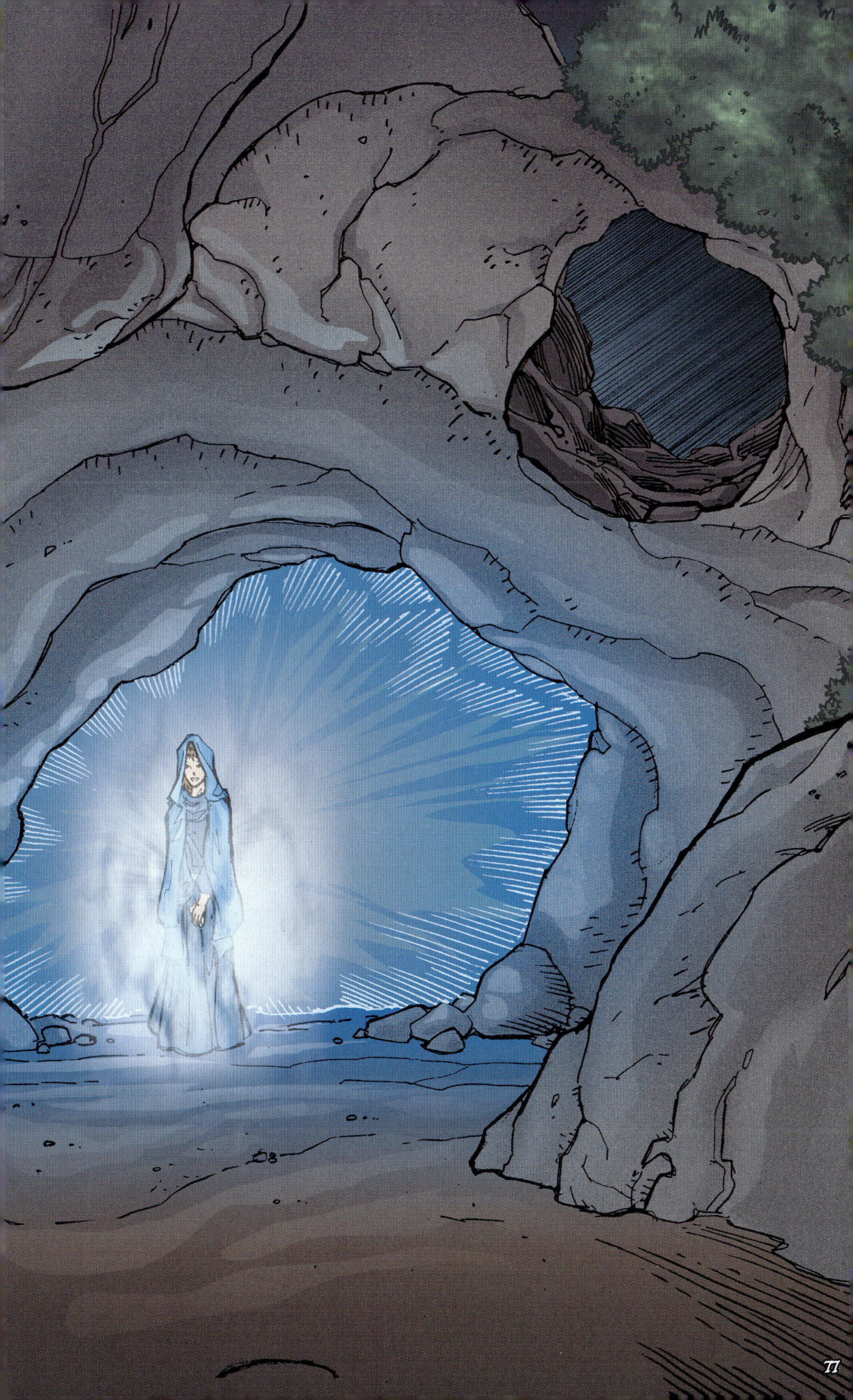

Come, child. Do not be afraid.
I AM NOT AFRAID, FOR YOUR SMILE IS THAT OF MY OWN MOTHER.
Truly, for I am a mother myself.
YOU ARE VERY BEAUTIFUL.
In Our Father's eyes, everyone is beautiful.
I KNOW IN MY HEART YOU SPEAK THE TRUTH, THOUGH WHEN I LOOK IN MY MIRROR IT IS HARDER TO BELIEVE. I LOOK AT YOU AND KNOW I HAVE NEVER SEEN ANYONE SO BEAUTIFUL.
YOU MUST BE AN ANGEL!
In time I will reveal my identity.
Keep faith, young child, for we will meet again.
THANK YOU. I WILL LOOK FOR YOU.
You must return home now, Bernadette.
ALREADY? BUT IT IS SO NICE TO BE HERE TALKING TO --
YOU.

LATER THAT NIGHT ...
YOU WERE GONE SO LONG TODAY, BERNADETTE. WHERE DID YOU EXPLORE?
ALL OVER, MY SISTER! ALL OVER.
I WISH I COULD EXPLORE. I WILL BE EIGHT SOON, YOU KNOW.
IT IS SO VERY HARD TO BE PATIENT. BUT IT IS WORTH IT; THE MYSTERIES OF GOD'S WORLD ASTOUNDED ME TODAY. YOU WOULD NEVER BELIEVE WHAT I SAW.
WHAT? WHAT DID YOU SEE?
OF THAT I AM NOT CERTAIN, THOUGH I KNOW IT WAS TRULY A MIRACLE!
I WISH I COULD SEE A MIRACLE ...
YOU MAKE ME LAUGH!
I WISH YOU COULD SEE, TOO. BUT I HAVE THIS FEELING IN MY HEART THAT I MAY BE THE ONLY ONE WHO CAN SEE FOR NOW ...
TIME TO SLEEP. GOODNIGHT.
GOODNIGHT!
I WISH I COULD HAVE BLOWN OUT THE CANDLE.

A FEW WEEKS LATER...

BERNADETTE -- ARE YOU GOING TO THE GROTTO? DO YOU THINK YOU WILL SEE HER?

I DON'T KNOW, MOTHER!

BUT I AM GOING. THOUGH I NEVER KNOW THE DAY, SHE CONTINUES TO COME TO ME, AND THE LADY IS ALWAYS SO BEAUTIFUL AND KIND.

I MUST RETURN TO THE GROTTO!

LORD, HOW COULD I EVER THANK YOU FOR THIS BLESSING? AND TO COME THROUGH BERNADETTE, OF ALL THE GIRLS IN FRANCE!

IN YOUR WISDOM, YOU HAVE CHOSEN THE MOST HUMBLE AND SIMPLE SPIRIT TO REVEAL YOURSELF TO. HOW COULD I HAVE QUESTIONED YOU?

FORGIVE ME, LORD, FOR DOUBTING YOU IN TIMES OF DARKNESS --

I KNOW THE TRUTH NOW, LORD. WHERE YOUR LIGHT SHINES, THERE IS ALWAYS HOPE.

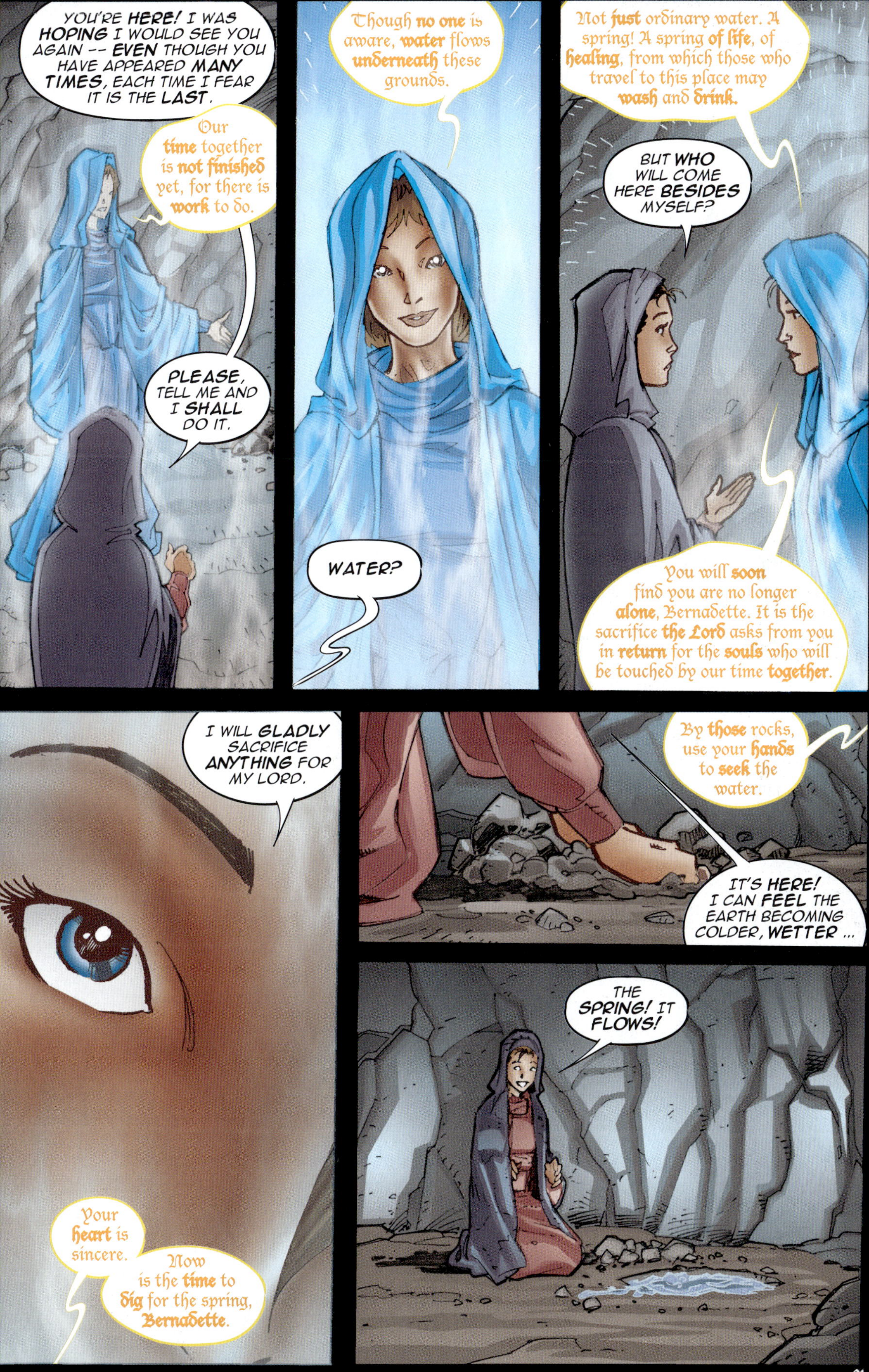
YOU'RE HERE! I WAS HOPING I WOULD SEE YOU AGAIN -- EVEN THOUGH YOU HAVE APPEARED MANY TIMES, EACH TIME I FEAR IT IS THE LAST.
Our time together is not finished yet, for there is work to do.
PLEASE, TELL ME AND I SHALL DO IT.
Though no one is aware, water flows underneath these grounds.
WATER?
Not just ordinary water. A spring! A spring of life, of healing, from which those who travel to this place may wash and drink.
BUT WHO WILL COME HERE BESIDES MYSELF?
You will soon find you are no longer alone, Bernadette. It is the sacrifice the Lord asks from you in return for the souls who will be touched by our time together.
I WILL GLADLY SACRIFICE ANYTHING FOR MY LORD.
Your heart is sincere.
Now is the time to dig for the spring, Bernadette.
By those rocks, use your hands to seek the water.
IT'S HERE! I CAN FEEL THE EARTH BECOMING COLDER, WETTER ...
THE SPRING! IT FLOWS!

A FEW WEEKS LATER...

ARE YOU SURE THIS IS THE SPOT THE VISION INSTRUCTED?

YES, KIND BUILDER, I HAVE ALREADY RELAYED THE MESSAGE TO YOU. DO NOT DOUBT ME. THE VISION TOLD ME TO BUILD A CHAPEL ON THIS VERY SITE, WHERE PILGRIMS MAY COME TO SEEK THE LORD. THEY WILL WASH AND DRINK FROM THE SPRING.

BUT YOU DON'T EVEN KNOW WHO SHE IS!

THE VISION HAS REVEALED THESE MIRACLES, AND I HAVE REVEALED THEM TO YOU. SHE HAS NOT YET SPOKEN OF HER IDENTITY.

PLEASE, REALIZE THAT IT IS NOT I WITH THE ANSWERS, BUT THE LORD HIMSELF.

SHE IS TIRED; YOU CAN SEE IT IN HER EYES. HER LUNGS ARE WEAK...

IT CANNOT BE EASY. SHE BEARS MUCH WEIGHT.

PERHAPS THE JOB HER FATHER HAS RECEIVED WILL LIGHTEN THE LOAD.

INDEED.

I HAVE HEARD THAT WITH HIS RECENT EARNINGS, BERNADETTE'S FATHER WAS ABLE TO PURCHASE THE FAMILY A HOUSE.

AND RIGHTLY SO, FOR NONE COULD STAND FOR SUCH A WOMAN OF GOD TO LIVE IN A BASEMENT FULL OF RATS AND STALE AIR.

SUCH A HOME WAS NOT FIT FOR OUR BERNADETTE.

HER VISIONS HAVE BROUGHT US MUCH HOPE, AND HEALING.

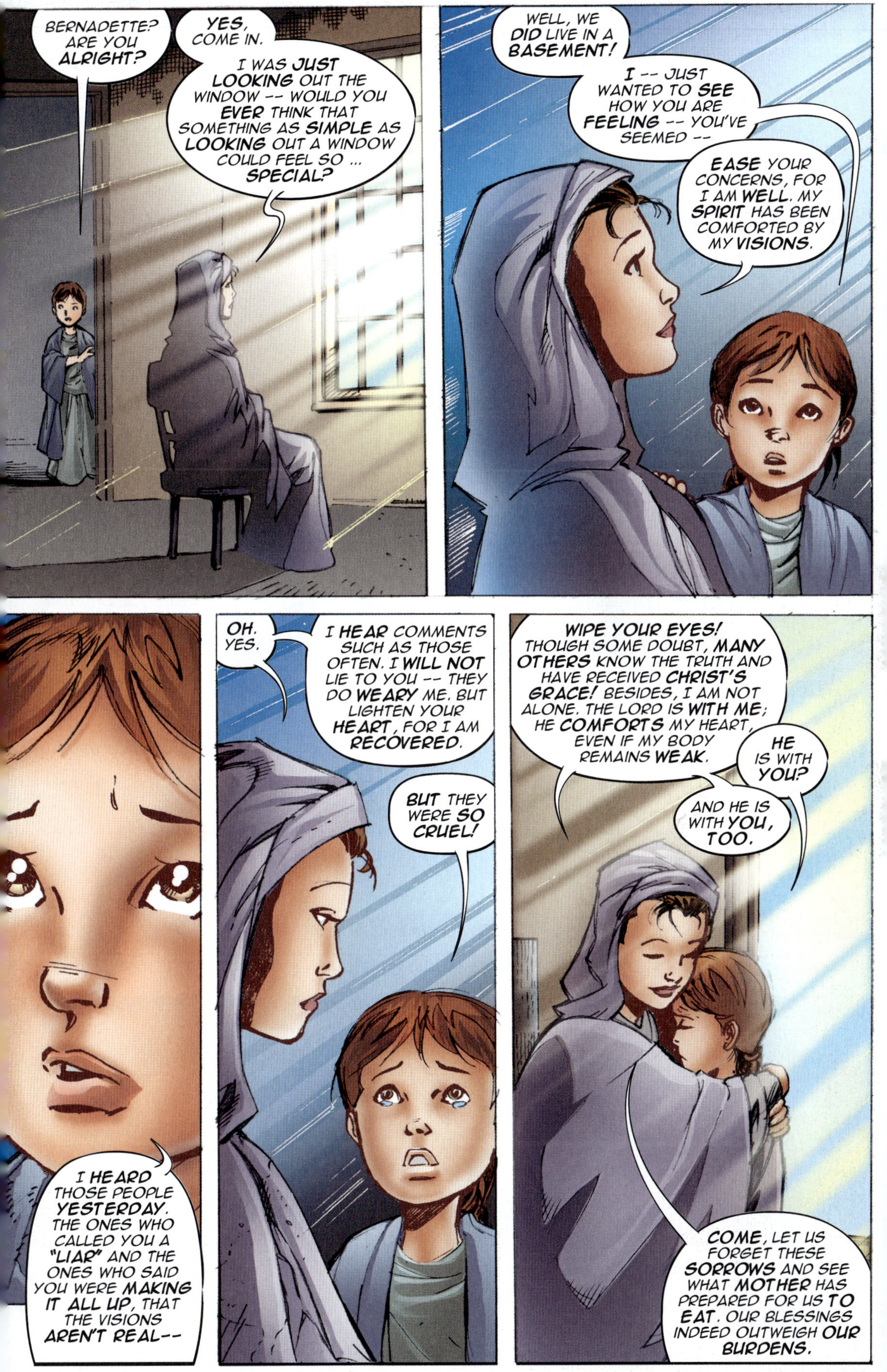
BERNADETTE? ARE YOU ALRIGHT?
YES, COME IN.
I WAS JUST LOOKING OUT THE WINDOW -- WOULD YOU EVER THINK THAT SOMETHING AS SIMPLE AS LOOKING OUT A WINDOW COULD FEEL SO ... SPECIAL?
WELL, WE DID LIVE IN A BASEMENT!
I -- JUST WANTED TO SEE HOW YOU ARE FEELING -- YOU'VE SEEMED --
EASE YOUR CONCERNS, FOR I AM WELL. MY SPIRIT HAS BEEN COMFORTED BY MY VISIONS.
I HEARD THOSE PEOPLE YESTERDAY. THE ONES WHO CALLED YOU A "LIAR" AND THE ONES WHO SAID YOU WERE MAKING IT ALL UP, THAT THE VISIONS AREN'T REAL--
OH. YES.
I HEAR COMMENTS SUCH AS THOSE OFTEN. I WILL NOT LIE TO YOU -- THEY DO WEARY ME. BUT LIGHTEN YOUR HEART, FOR I AM RECOVERED.
BUT THEY WERE SO CRUEL!
WIPE YOUR EYES! THOUGH SOME DOUBT, MANY OTHERS KNOW THE TRUTH AND HAVE RECEIVED CHRIST'S GRACE! BESIDES, I AM NOT ALONE. THE LORD IS WITH ME; HE COMFORTS MY HEART, EVEN IF MY BODY REMAINS WEAK.
HE IS WITH YOU?
AND HE IS WITH YOU, TOO.
COME, LET US FORGET THESE SORROWS AND SEE WHAT MOTHER HAS PREPARED FOR US TO EAT. OUR BLESSINGS INDEED OUTWEIGH OUR BURDENS.

MARCH 25TH.

Hello, child.

I THOUGHT FOR A MOMENT YOU WEREN'T GOING TO APPEAR.

The chapel is built, and the spring flows, healing many.

Be consoled, for I am here.

SO MANY GOOD THINGS HAVE HAPPENED. PEOPLE FLOCK TO THE CHAPEL IN THOUSANDS; THEY FOLLOW ME HERE, TO THIS PLACE, IN HOPES THEY, TOO, MIGHT GLIMPSE YOUR FACE.

AND MY FAMILY ... SO MANY SORROWS HAVE BEEN LIFTED.

Yes, there is hope to be found in this place.

Bernadette, I have to come to finally reveal to you, at last, my identity.

PLEASE, TELL ME, LADY, WHO IS IT THAT HAS CHANGED MY LIFE AND TOUCHED THE PEOPLE OF FRANCE?

I am the Immaculate Conception.
MARY, THE MOTHER OF JESUS! OUR LADY!
AND SO THE VISIONS CONTINUED TO COME TO BERNADETTE UNTIL JULY OF THAT SUMMER, WHEN THEY CEASED, LEAVING BEHIND THE MIRACULOUS SPRING WHOSE WATERS HEALED MANY AND A CHAPEL THAT BECKONED PILGRIMS FROM COUNTRIES ALL OVER THE WORLD.
BUT WHAT WAS ALSO LEFT BEHIND WAS A YOUNG GIRL, WHOSE LIFE HAD BEEN CHANGED AND WHOSE FUTURE SEEMED UNCERTAIN.

SIX YEARS LATER ...

JUST DON'T LISTEN, DON'T LISTEN ...

LORD, GIVE ME STRENGTH!

WHY DON'T YOU STOP TO SPEAK WITH US, BERNADETTE -- OR ARE YOUR EARS TOO HOLY TO RECEIVE THE WORDS OF MERE MORTALS?

TELL ME, BERNADETTE -- WHY DID THE VISIONS STOP? IS IT BECAUSE YOUR FATHER HAD ALREADY BOUGHT HIS HOUSE?!

SHE HAS ALWAYS BEEN SO ILL -- HOW COULD SHE EVEN KNOW WHAT SHE WAS SEEING -- IF SHE WAS IN FACT SEEING ANYTHING AT ALL?

TELL ME, BERNADETTE, DID THE MIRACLE SPRING HEAL YOUR ASTHMA?

MOTHER ... HELP ...

BERNADETTE, IS THAT YOU? BERNADETTE -- ARE YOU ALRIGHT?!

FRANCOIS, COME QUICKLY!

SHE IS RESTING NOW. THANK GOD SHE HAD ARRIVED HOME. I DON'T WANT TO IMAGINE WHAT COULD HAVE HAPPENED --

PEACE, MY LOVE. NOTHING DID HAPPEN. SHE IS HERE; SHE IS WELL.

WHEN IT IS NOT THE ONES TAUNTING HER, IT IS THE ONES WORSHIPPING HER, ASKING HER INNUMERABLE QUESTIONS, BEGGING FOR PIECES OF HER CLOTHING AS RELICS.

STILL, MY MIND CANNOT ESCAPE THE "WHAT IF" ...

SHE DOES NOT REVEAL IT, BUT HER HEART IS SORE WITH PAIN. THE NEWSPAPERS QUESTION HER VISIONS --

WHILE HER SUPPORTERS WILL NOT CEASE INVADING HER PRIVACY.

I LONG TO COMFORT HER -- MY HEART YEARNS TO GRANT HER PEACE.

MOTHER, FATHER --

HOW ARE YOU FEELING?

CAN WE DO ANYTHING?

PLEASE --

I HAVE PRAYED OVER THE ADVICE GIVEN TO ME ...

I KNOW NOW WHAT I MUST DO.

COME NOW, CHILDREN. IT IS TIME TO SAY --
GOODBYE.
DON'T GO!
OH, DO NOT CRY! NO -- THIS IS A HAPPY DAY, TRULY.
IT IS FOR THE BEST THAT I LEAVE FOR THE SISTERS OF NOTRE-DAME DE NEVERS. THERE MY BODY CAN FINALLY REST.
BUT WHAT ABOUT US?
I WILL MISS YOU ALL UNBEARABLY. THAT IS CERTAIN.
BUT KNOW THIS -- YOU WILL ALWAYS BE IN MY PRAYERS.
NO MATTER WHERE I AM.

Sudden Celebrity

SOUBIROUS FAMILY BIRTHS A GIRL

January 7, 1844
Marie Bernadette, commonly called "Bernadette", is born to parents Francois Soubirous and Louise Casterot. She is the eldest of six children in the family.

1844
Bernadette's father rents a mill of his own to support his family.

CHOLERA EPIDEMIC SWEEPS FRANCE

1854
A cholera epidemic sweeps France, affecting Bernadette's already weak health permanently. Meanwhile, the family is sinking into debt and poverty. During this time, Bernadette's father must give up the mill and the family moves into the basement of a rundown building. Bernadette is unable to attend school or receive her First Communion due to her family's financial state and her compromised health.

February 11, 1858
Bernadette receives her first vision at Lourdes. The series of visions lasts a few months and then ceases. During this time the people of France take great interest in the visions and assist Bernadette's father in finding work. Bernadette is immediately a public figure and plagued with the ramifications of celebrity. Thousands flock to Lourdes for its miraculous healing waters.

1861-1866
Due to the intensive attention from those seeking to question and interview Bernadette, as well as desiring her to bless them or their families and grant them relics, Bernadette resides with nuns at a hospice. However, even there the young girl is unable to deny certain visitors. Though she suffers greatly from physical pain, Bernadette answers visitors' questions with pleasant and endless patience.

1866
After delays due to sickness, Bernadette is finally able to join the sisters of Notre-Dame de Nevers, her character ever humble and patient. Only four months after her arrival, Bernadette becomes gravely ill and is considered on her death bed, receiving the final sacraments. However, she soon recovers, and resumes helping the sick and administering ~~~~~ to others.

1876
The basilica at Lourdes is consecrated, though Bernadette voluntarily takes no part in the celebrations. It is later revealed that Bernadette secretly wished to see the consecration, but could not allow herself to be noticed publicly.

April 16, 1879
Bernadette passes away at the age of thirty-five.

1933
Bernadette is canonized officially as St. Mary Bernarda, but is widely known as St. Bernadette. Pilgrims still to this day gather at the grotto of Massablielle, seeking the healing powers of the Lourdes spring.

Would you give up your life for Christ?

Saint Charles Lwanga

Saint Charles Lwanga

CHARLES LWANGA, ALSO KNOWN AS **KALOLI LWANGA,** IS BORN IN **1860** IN THE COUNTRY OF **UGANDA,** LOCATED IN EAST SUB-SAHARAN AFRICA. HE IS A MEMBER OF THE BUSH-BUCK, OR **NGABI,** CLAN OF THE GANDA PEOPLE.

THE SOCIETY OF MISSIONARIES OF **OUR LADY OF THE AFRICAN MISSIONS** ARRIVES IN UGANDA IN 1879. CHARLES BECOMES VERY INTERESTED IN THEIR TEACHINGS, AND BEGINS TO ATTEND THEIR INSTRUCTIONS.

A CHARMING MAN, LIKED BY ALL, CHARLES JOINS THE COURT OF **KING MWANGA** IN 1884 AND IS QUICKLY PLACED IN COMMAND OF THE ROYAL PAGES OF THE GREAT AUDIENCE HALL. HE WINS THE CONFIDENCE OF HIS YOUNG CHARGES AND EXCELS IN **WRESTLING,** WHICH IS THE MOST POPULAR SPORT AT THE PALACE.

LIFE FOR CHARLES IS WELL, **FOR A TIME** -- UNTIL THE NEW KING'S VIOLENT TEMPER AND CRUELTY BECOMES EVIDENT TO ALL. IN THE SPAN OF A YEAR, THE KINGDOM HAD BECOMES A **DARK** AND **UNHOLY** PLACE.

IN THESE SURROUNDINGS, A MAN SUCH AS **CHARLES LWANGA** IS COMPELLED TO ACT.

PRODUCER: Daniel Burton

EDITORIAL: Kimberly Black

STORY: Terry Collins

PENCILS: Michael Patterson

INKS: Derek Fridolfs

COLORS: Carsten Bradley

LETTERS: Keith Bahrenburg

The Royal Palace of Uganda.

The living quarters of Charles Lwanga.

November 15, 1885. 3:45 p.m.

I HAD THE DREAM AGAIN LAST NIGHT, MKASA.

THE ONE OF DARKNESS AND FIRE?

YES -- TWO OF THE SAME DREAMS NOW IN A ROW.

I HAVE HAD THIS SAME VISION FOR AN ENTIRE WEEK NOW -- THAT IS A WARNING.

IS THIS YOUR WAY OF TELLING ME NOT TO SPEAK WITH THE KING, CHARLES?

YOU KNOW I ALWAYS WELCOME YOUR COUNSEL, MY FRIEND BUT --

THE DECISION IS YOURS AND YOURS ALONE TO MAKE, MKASA.

YES, I KNOW.

I FEAR JUST AS YOU DO FOR THE FUTURE OF UGANDA. KING MWANGA'S APPETITES GROW MORE DISHONORABLE EACH DAY.

I KNOW. THE ROYAL PAGES HAVE TOLD ME OF THE HARM HE HAS CAUSED THEM -- HIS CRUEL NATURE.

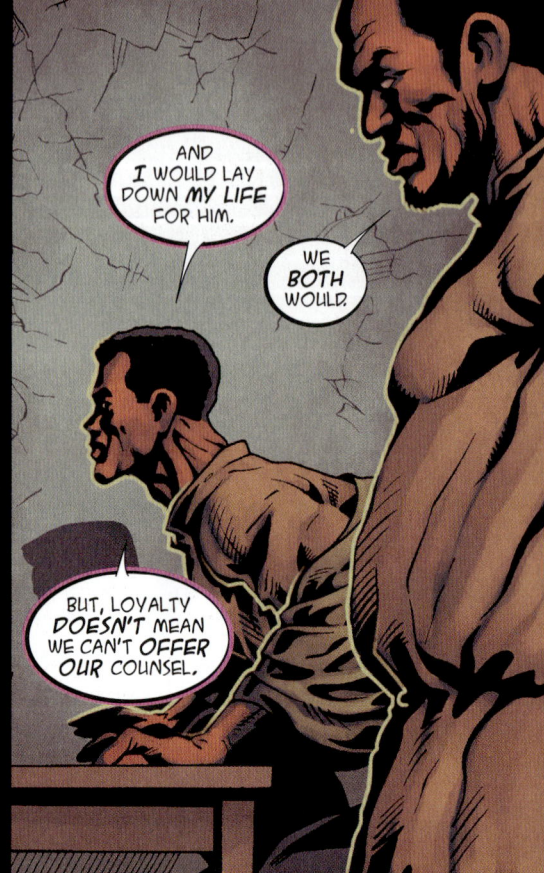

"YES, HE TREATS THE PAGES MOST *DISHONORABLY* -- THIS IS THE VERY REASON WE *CAN NOT* CONTINUE TO LET HIM DESTROY *INNOCENT* PEOPLE'S LIVES!"

"YES, BUT *THE KING* IS STILL MY FRIEND -- AND OUR KING."

"AND *I* WOULD LAY DOWN *MY LIFE* FOR HIM."

"WE *BOTH* WOULD."

"BUT, LOYALTY *DOESN'T* MEAN WE CAN'T *OFFER* OUR COUNSEL."

"I WILL *MEET* THE KING TONIGHT, CHARLES, AND I WILL *DISCUSS* THE WELFARE OF HIS PAGES, AND PROTEST *THE MURDER* OF A FELLOW CHRISTIAN."

"THE ANGLICAN MISSIONARY, BISHOP HANNINGTON, WAS *KILLED* THIS MORNING. I FIND MYSELF UNABLE TO *STAY SILENT* WITH THIS DEATH."

"SURELY THE KING KNOWS THIS *ACTION* WILL DRAW THE EYES OF *THE BRITISH GOVERNMENT* UPON HIM?"

"HE NO LONGER *CARES.* I FEAR HE HAS GONE *MAD* WITH *THE POWER* OF HIS POSITION."

"I HAD *NOT* HEARD."

WE BOTH KNOW THE INFLUENCE OF THE MISSIONARIES UPON THE KING'S COURT HAS FALLEN SINCE THE REIGN OF KING MUTESA -- MWANGA BARELY TOLERATES THEIR PRESENCE ANYMORE.
HE HEARS WHISPERS THAT THE MISSIONARIES ARE A THREAT TO HIS RULE AND --
IT IS CONVENIENT FOR HIM TO BELIEVE SUCH LIES, MKASA.
I KNOW THIS, BUT STILL, I MUST TRY AND REACH WHAT IS LEFT OF THE GOOD SOUL THAT IS STILL INSIDE OF HIM.
CHARLES, I HAVE COME TO RELY ON YOU FOR THE INSTRUCTION AND GUIDANCE OF THE KING'S PAGES --
AND FOR SHIELDING THEM FROM THE EVIL INFLUENCES AT COURT.
IF I DO NOT RETURN TONIGHT, THEN THEIR SAFETY AND WELFARE FALLS ENTIRELY UPON YOU.
I UNDERSTAND, MY FRIEND. I WILL PRAY FOR YOU.
NOT FOR ME, CHARLES. PRAY FOR OUR KABAKA -- PRAY FOR OUR KING.
I WILL PRAY FOR US ALL.

THESE MISSIONARIES, THEY SPEAK OF SNAKES DISGUISED AS FRIENDS, DO THEY NOT?

4:26 p.m.

SO IT IS WRITTEN IN THE HOLY BOOK.

THE BOOK OF THEIR GOD! SOON, THEY WILL NO LONGER BE WELCOME IN MY KINGDOM.

STILL, MY FEELINGS ARE NO SECRET -- NOR ARE YOUR OWN RELIGIOUS IDEALS.

WHAT DISGUISE DOES MY CHIEF STEWARD WEAR TODAY? IS HE A LAMB OR A SNAKE?

I WISH TO BEG THE KING FOR MERCY -- MERCY FOR HIMSELF AND MERCY FOR HIS PEOPLE.

YOUR DESIRES FRIGHTEN US ALL, KABAKA. THOSE WHO ATTEND YOU, YOUR PAGES, SHOULD NOT BE PREY TO YOUR UNHOLY WISHES.

THEY SHOULD NOT BE TREATED AS YOU ARE TREATING THEM NOW! THIS CRUELTY CAN NOT GO ON ANY LONGER!

MY PAGES ARE HERE TO SERVE THEIR KING, AND WILL OBEY MY COMMANDS -- ALL OF MY COMMANDS.

BUT YOUR COMMANDS -- THEY ARE AN ABOMINATION! YOU MUST CHANGE YOUR WAYS, KING MWANGA! YOU MUST REPENT BEFORE IT IS TOO LATE.

MKASA, I HAVE ALWAYS LIKED YOU. AND SO, I HAVE INDULGED YOUR DABBLINGS IN THIS CHRISTIANITY.
BUT BE WARNED -- OUR LONG FRIENDSHIP DOES NOT GRANT YOU THE RIGHT TO TELL A KABAKA WHAT TO DO.
MY GOD TELLS ME WHAT I MUST SAY. I AM BUT A VESSEL FOR HIS WORDS AND --
ENOUGH!

IT SEEMS MY GOD HAS SHIFTED YOUR AIM, KING MWANGA.
GUARDS, TAKE THIS TRAITOR! HE SHALL PERISH BEFORE SUNSET!
5:09 p.m.
THERE IS NO NEED TO BIND ME. I STAND READY.
A MAN WHO GIVES HIS LIFE FOR GOD IS NOT AFRAID TO DIE.
OUR KING HAS CONDEMNED ME WITHOUT CAUSE, BUT I FORGIVE HIM --
FROM MY HEART.

6:35 p.m.
CHARLES! CHARLES! COME QUICKLY!
WHAT IS WRONG, CHILDREN?
IT'S MKASA -- HE'S, HE'S --
-- DEAD.
THEN IT HAS BEGUN.
PAGES! ATTEND ME -- WE SHALL SEEK THE COUNSEL OF FATHER LOURDEL.
The Catholic Mission.
7:40 p.m.
ENTER, MY SONS. I HAVE ALREADY BEEN TOLD OF MKASA'S PASSING.
YOU MAY STAY AS LONG AS YOU LIKE, CHARLES. THE HOUSE OF THE LORD IS ALWAYS OPEN.
I HAVE CONTINUOUSLY FOUND HAVEN IN THE CHURCH, FATHER, BUT EVEN HERE WE ARE NOT SAFE FROM THE RAGE OF KING MWANGA.

WHAT ELSE CAN I DO FOR YOU ON THIS TERRIBLE NIGHT?
THESE YOUNG ONES NEED TO RECEIVE HOLY BAPTISM, FATHER. WILL YOU DO THIS FOR US?
I WOULD BE HONORED.
I BAPTIZE THEE IN THE NAME OF THE FATHER, AND OF THE SON, AND OF THE HOLY SPIRIT.
10:01 p.m.
THE BOYS ARE FINALLY ASLEEP, CHARLES. I DID NOT THINK KIZITO WOULD EVER STOP TALKING.
THEY ARE VERY BRAVE. THEY RECEIVED THE SACRAMENT OF REGENERATION WITH WONDERFUL FAITH.
ALL THE MORE INSPIRING THEN, SINCE THEY MAY SOON SEAL IT WITH THEIR OWN LIVES.

Six Months Later --

The Royal Court of Uganda.

The sleeping quarters of Charles Lwanga.

May 6, 1886. 5:38 a.m.

LWANGA! YOU ARE SUMMONED!

HIS EXCELLENCY DEMANDS YOUR PRESENCE -- NOW!

CHARLES, I HAVE BEEN *KIND* TO YOU, HAVE I NOT? YET WHEN I *DEMAND* FOR YOU TO END THIS *RELIGIOUS FOOLISHNESS*, YOU CONTINUE TO GO *BEHIND MY BACK*.

I'VE BEEN *ASKING* YOU FOR MONTHS TO *STOP*. WHAT *SAY* YOU TODAY?

I *SAY* THAT THOUGH YOU ARE MY *KABAKA*, AND I STAND READY TO *DIE* TO *PROTECT* YOU -- I CANNOT DENY MY *LORD JESUS CHRIST*.

YOU SHOULD *KNOW*, CHARLES, THAT I NOW HAVE *THE CONSENT* OF MY CHIEFTAINS TO *RID MYSELF* ENTIRELY OF ANY CHRISTIANS IN *MY COURT*.

WHY DO YOU *FEAR* OUR *GOD* SO MUCH, MY *KING*?

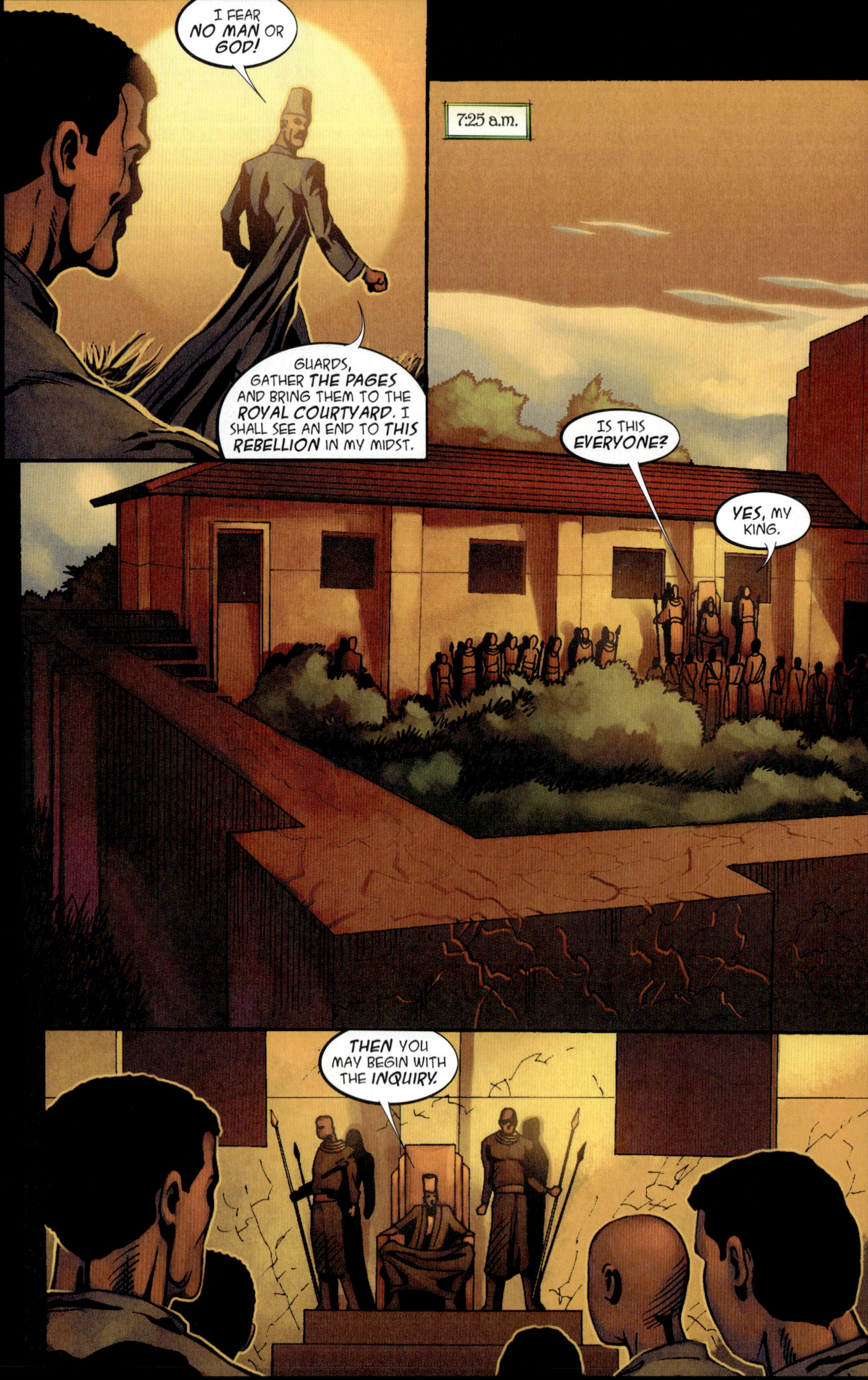
I FEAR NO MAN OR GOD!
GUARDS, GATHER THE PAGES AND BRING THEM TO THE ROYAL COURTYARD. I SHALL SEE AN END TO THIS REBELLION IN MY MIDST.
7:25 a.m.
IS THIS EVERYONE?
YES, MY KING.
THEN YOU MAY BEGIN WITH THE INQUIRY.

PAGES OF THE COURT -- YOU HAVE BEEN SUMMONED BY EDICT OF THE KING FOR ONE REASON, AND ONE REASON ONLY.
ALL THOSE WHO PRAY TO JESUS CHRIST -- CONFESS YOUR FAITH!
WE ARE ALL CHRISTIANS HERE!
AND DO YOU INTEND TO REMAIN CHRISTIANS?
UNTIL DEATH!
UNTIL DEATH.
SO BE IT.
I SENTENCE YOU ALL TO THE DEATH YOU SO WELCOME!

9:00 a.m.
CHARLES, I AM DISMAYED AT THESE ACTIONS. WHY WOULD MWANGA SENTENCE THESE CHILDREN TO SUCH A FATE?
MY KING THINKS THIS IS PUNISHMENT, BUT HE IS WRONG.
DO NOT LOOK SAD, FATHER. WE WALK THIS PATH WITH JOY IN OUR HEARTS.
IT IS TIME.
THIS EARTH IS NOTHING TO THE DELIGHTS YOU HAVE TAUGHT US TO LOOK FORWARD TO IN HEAVEN.
I SHALL PLEAD YOUR CASE BEFORE THE KING, AND BEG FOR MERCY.
DO NOT PLACE YOURSELF IN HARM'S WAY BY RISKING THE KING'S ALREADY FEROCIOUS ANGER.
WE GO TO A BETTER PLACE!
YOU SHALL NOT BE FORGOTTEN, CHARLES. YOUR NAMES AND DEEDS WILL OUTLIVE US ALL.

May 8, 1886. 2:37 p.m.
WHERE ARE WE MARCHING TO, CHARLES?
WE'VE BEEN WALKING FOR TWO DAYS NOW, WITH NO WATER OR FOOD.
WE GO TO NAMUGONGO, MBAGA.
THIS FOOLISHNESS HAS GONE ON LONG ENOUGH. RENOUNCE YOUR FAITH AND LET ME TAKE YOU BACK HOME, MBAGA.
I LOVE YOU FATHER, BUT MY FATHER WHOM I MUST NOW OBEY IS IN HEAVEN.
PLEASE, MY SON. ONCE WE ARE IN NAMUGONGO, IT WILL BE TOO LATE.
EVEN I, AS CHIEF EXECUTIONER, WILL BE UNABLE TO STOP YOUR DEATH.
FATHER, DO NOT BE AFRAID -- FOR I AM NOT FRIGHTENED.

June 3, 1886. 8:00 a.m.
Namugongo.
IT IS TIME.
WHERE IS YOUR GOD NOW?
HE IS ALL AROUND US, SENKOLE.
MY GOD AND THE GOD OF YOUR SON, HE HAS NEVER LEFT US.

YOU KNOW THIS IS YOUR FAULT, CHARLES LWANGA. THEY ARE ALL BLINDED, JUST AS MY SON MBAGA IS, BY YOUR TEACHINGS.
MY SON MUST DIE BY ORDER OF THE KING --

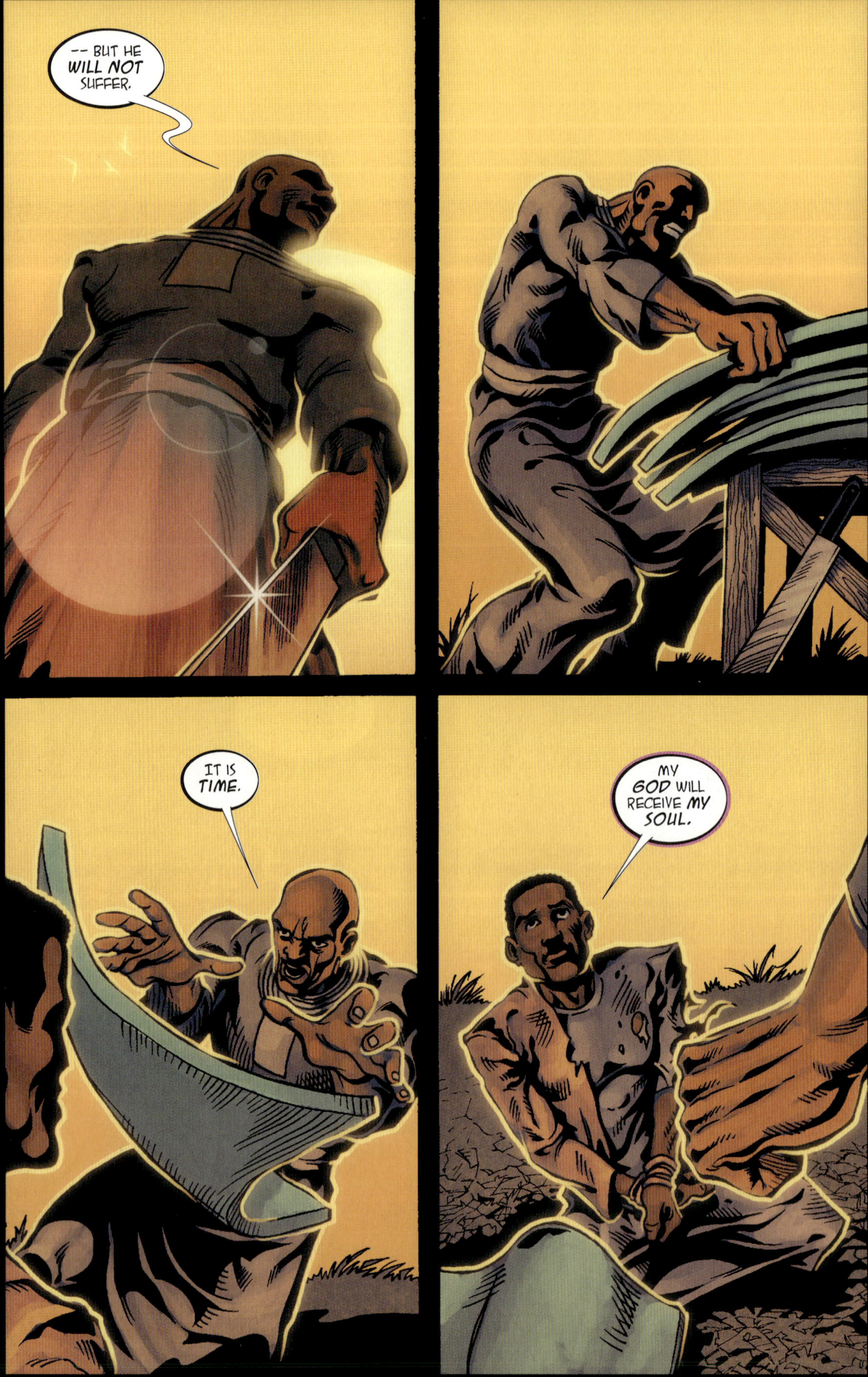
-- BUT HE WILL NOT SUFFER.
IT IS TIME.
MY GOD WILL RECEIVE MY SOUL.

FOR GOD HAS RESCUED ME, AND I WILL BE WITH HIM IN HEAVEN THIS VERY DAY.
MY FRIENDS, WE SHALL BEFORE LONG MEET AGAIN IN HEAVEN.
MBAGA WAS THE FIRST TO GO TO GLORY TODAY -- AND NOW, I GO ON AHEAD OF YOU.
KATONDA!*
KEEP YOUR COURAGE, AND PERSEVERE TO THE END!
* Katonda = My God

Charles Lwanga is declared "Blessed," along with twenty-one other Ugandan martyrs by Pope Benedict XV in 1920.

Pope Paul VI canonizes all twenty-two in 1964.

In 1969, Paul VI personally lays the foundation stone of the Catholic shrine at Namugongo, on the place of St. Charles Lwanga's martyrdom.

A Saint's Journey

- **January 1, 1860**
  CHARLES LWANGA IS BORN KALOLI LWANGA

- **November 15, 1885**
  LWANGA IS BAPTIZED BY PERE GIRAUD ON THE SAME DAY KING MWANGA BEHEADS JOSEPH MKASA.

- **May 27, 1886**
  THREE YOUTHS ARE KILLED ON THE 37 MILE TREK TO NAMUGONGO.

- **June 3, 1886**
  ASCENSION DAY—CHARLES LWANGA AND THE REMAINING BOYS ARE SET ALIGHT ON A PYRE. LWANGA IS SET APART FOR PRIVATE EXECUTION.

- **1920**
  CHARLES LWANGA, ANDREW KAGWA, MATTHIAS MURUMBA, AND 19 OTHERS ARE BEATIFIED.

- **October 18, 1964**
  THE MARTYRS ARE CANONIZED BY POPE PAUL VI.

GO!
Make disciples of all nations.

Baptize them in the name of the Father, the Son, and the Holy Spirit.

Teach them to obey everything I have commanded you.

Matthew 28:19-20a

*GO! Make disciples of all nations.

Baptize them in the name of the Father, the Son, and the Holy Spirit.

Teach them to obey everything I have commanded you.

Matthew 28:19-20a